Self and School Success

SUNY Series, Studying the Self
Richard P. Lipka and Thomas M. Brinthaupt, editors

and

SUNY Series, Student Lore: The Educational Experience of
Students in School and Society
William H. Schubert, Editor

Self and School Sucess

Voices and Lore of Inner-City Students

Edwin William Farrell

STATE UNIVERSITY OF NEW YORK PRESS

Published by
State University of New York Press

Printed in the United State of America

For information, address the State University of New York Press,
State University Plaza, Albany, NY 12246

Library of Congress Cataloging-in-Publication Data

Farrell, Edwin William.
    Self and school success : voices and lore of inner-city students /
Edwin Farrell.
        p.   cm. -- (SUNY series, studying the self)   (SUNY series,
student lore)
    Includes bibliographical references (p.) and index.
    ISBN 0-7914-1845-6 (alk. paper). -- ISBN 0-7914-1846-4 (pbk. :
alk. paper)
    1. Socially handicapped children--New York (N.Y.)--Attitudes.
    2. Socially handicapped children--Education--New York (N.Y.)
    3. Socially handicapped children--New York (N.Y.)--Interviews.
    4. Identity (Psychology)   5. Ego (Psychology)   6. Eductional
surveys--New York (N.Y.)   I. Title.   II. Series.   III. Series: SUNY
series, student lore.
LC4091.F37   1994
371.96 '7 '097471--dc20   93-10229
                                                            CIP

10 9 8 7 6 5 4 3 2 1

Contents

Series Editor's Foreword

No voice has been more neglected in the quest to improve education than the voice of students. This is patently ironic in view of the fact that students are the most important group in the education enterprise. Students are its reason for being.

Edwin Farrell gave insight into at-risk students in his earlier book, *Hanging In and Dropping Out,* using a unique method of inquiry that engaged high school students as collaborators and interviewers. Through this earlier book, he illuminated the voices of at-risk high school students in New York City. In *Self and School Success* Farrell builds on the substance and method of inquiry in his previous book—this time focusing on students in inner-city schools who have been successful. This is, indeed, a contribution to "student lore." The voices of students, the contextual portrayals, and the commentary provided by Farrell will provoke insight, reflection, controversy, and debate. That is the essence of what a good book should do.

I hope this book will encourage others to creatively portray the voices of students. We need to know more about how students experience education and how they reflect on that experience, as John Dewey has long taught us (e.g., Dewey 1938). This pertains to experience that occurs out-of-school as well as in-school. *Student Lore* should give attention to diverse groups of students— such as students of different settings (urban, rural, suburban), places, ethnicities, social classes, genders, races, states of health and ableness, appearance, and other dimensions. There is a great poverty of opportunity for student voices to be heard. Edwin Farrell offers a worthy contribution toward the great task of over-coming this deficit.

The Student Lore Series is designed to give audience to the voice of students. Good teachers have taught us that they turn to the insights of students to guide their teaching (see *Teacher Lore* by Schubert and Ayers, 1992). Following the example of good teachers who seek to better understand their students' lives, both in and out of school, we want to encourage researchers, teachers, and students themselves to write about the educational experiences of students.

William H. Schubert
Editor

To Sean and Shane
Sons and Students

Acknowledgments

A number of people were essential to the preparation of this book. First, I would like to thank the four young women who collected the data for the study by interviewing their fellow high school students in places and situations where I could not: Stephanie Henry, then at Grover Cleveland High School; Johanna Montesano, then at John F. Kennedy High School; and Rosa Angel Perez and Betzayada Lozado, then at the High School of Telecommunications, Art, and Technology.

Next, I owe a great debt to the three of their teachers—and my graduate students—who recruited them: Neifi Acosta, John D. Wells Junior High School; Ronald Gerner, Adlai E. Stevenson High School; and Stephen White, Grover Cleveland High School; all employees of the New York City Board of Education.

The data that inform chapter 5, a study of parental attitudes, were collected by Leslie Hall, Angela Hernandez, and Raymond Nazario, teachers for the New York City Board of Education and my graduate students and collaborators at the City College. Angela was able to interview parents in Spanish and translate the material into English for purposes of transcription.

Johanna Young transcribed the data for the student and the parent studies, changing dialogue to text, an excruciating and an always underrewarded task.

The data that inform chapter 7, a study of teacher attitudes, were collected and transcribed by Catherine deMare, Miguel Esper, Janett Gonzalez, and, again, Angela Hernandez. The aforementioned were also both teachers for the New York City Board of Education and my graduate students at the City College. I thank them for their wisdom and their long hours of work.

The research project was partly supported by a grant from the Research Foundation of the City University of New York (PSC-CUNY, 1990–91). The CUNY Research Foundation, in the person of Ethel Breheny, was always available for help.

Leslie Alexander and Sid Massey, director and acting director of River East Elementary School made it possible for me to observe the wonders of their school. Sonia Bailey did the same in Central Park East Secondary.

For those incidental hallway conversations that stimulate ideas like nothing else, I owe much to my colleagues in the erstwhile Department of Social and

Psychological Foundations at the City College. In particular, I would like to thank Irvin Schonfeld, who keeps me honest as a researcher, and Harwood Fisher, who keeps me thinking.

Finally, I would like to thank Lois Patton at the State University of New York Press who believed in my idea and Bill Schubert of the University of Illinois, Chicago, the editor of the series of which this book is a part, who believed in the finished product.

Introduction

Anthony: I love school and I don't care who hears this; I am in love with school because it gets what I want done fast.

Natalia: The teachers are really good...they are. Some teachers, you know, they're human, Everybody has their bad days, but the majority of teachers are really good....

This is a book about young women and young men who succeed in school. These young people attend inner-city high schools; virtually all are members of minority groups and are from poor or working-class homes. They are in the process of discovering who they are and where they will fit in. Every day they encounter and overcome problems endemic to cities: drugs, violence, declining economic conditions. Gaining insight on how they do this by listening to their voices is the goal of this book.

The problems of American education today are often seen to be greatest in urban areas. The decline of a manufacturing job base, the redistribution of income, the drying up of government funding for schools, changes in demographic patterns due to immigration and middle-class flight from the cities, and a declining tax base for local expenditures have put pressures on urban school systems which they can barely withstand. The results of these pressures—overcrowding, racial incidents, violence, drug use, low achievement, and high dropout rates—have made some city schools nightmares.

To a lesser extent, however, the same economic problems impact on schools in suburbs, in small towns, and even in rural areas. We hear that American students are not up to snuff compared with their peers in other industrialized countries. While not all our communities can become like Garrison Keillor's Lake Woebegone ("where all the children are above average"), they can aspire to educate their youth so that they all, at least, get a fair start and have reasonable expectations in the pursuit of happiness.

All educators and parents want to see their children succeed in school. But success, in this context, does not necessarily mean a report card full of A's or a high score on a standardized test. It means success as far as the student is concerned: mastery of the basic tools of her technology, becoming part of social groups, integration into the greater society, a vision of a happy and

1

productive future. But in a society that demands credentials, young people must be able to earn the basic credential. The high school diploma seems to be that credential. Most jobs demand it; it is the eligibility requirement for admission to many civil service examinations, the armed forces, and, of course, higher education. And there is an implied belief among educators that the high school diploma cannot be beyond the abilities of most of our students. If it were, there would be no dropout "problem"; dropping out would be expected.

This is not to say that diplomas should be given away. Elsewhere I have written about special education students I taught who earned high school diplomas. I think of one, Dale, who drives a truck, owns a home, has a circle of friends, pays taxes, and appears to be happy. He succeeded in school according to the criteria listed in the paragraph above. His transcript does not read the same as that of his classmate who went to Dartmouth but Dale learned enough of the tools of his technology to be integrated into the greater society.

What is it, we ask as educators, that accounts for the success of Dale and his college-bound classmate? Both lived in a pleasant town in coastal Maine. More to our concern, however, is the question, what is it that accounts for the success of those students who graduate high school while living in conditions far removed from the American dream? If we can account for their academic success, we may be able to account for academic success in general.

Furthermore, if we account for success *from their points of view*, we should be able to propose educational environments that would be conducive to academic success. Some such environments already exist, I think; others would have to be created. The creation of new environments, new schools, or new programs within existing schools must be built on student success but not success as measured by tests or by how many years of Latin students take and, especially, not by how many of a particular graduating class attend college. We must begin by reinforcing what *in them* accounts for their success.

IDENTITY FORMATION AND ADOLESCENT SELVES

To arrive at what accounts for success, I would like to proceed under the rubric of what Jerome Bruner (1990) calls "cultural psychology," in which participating people can agree on their interpretation of what they say and do and of the situations in which these sayings and doings occur. But because it is helpful to have a theoretical framework when looking at what is *in* the adolescent, I will synthesize some of the developmental theories of Erik Erikson (1963) and, more importantly, Harry Stack Sullivan (1953), along with the social construction theories of Peter Berger and Thomas Luckmann (1967).

The concept most identified with Erikson is that of "ego identity." To Erikson, the ego is the central principle of organization within the individual; it must integrate growth with the structure of social institutions. Identity is a quality of the ego that develops in stages over the life span but which he believes crystallizes largely during the critical period of adolescence. It answers the questions: "Who am I?" (in terms of my social role); "Where do I fit in?"; "What is my future occupational role?" From their sociological point of view, Berger and Luckmann define identity as "the total self" (p. 91).

Harry Stack Sullivan's (1953) concept of the "self system" can be considered as a parallel to Erikson's ego identity. This self system is created and recreated in all our interpersonal relationships throughout the life span. For Sullivan, there is a self for every other self that we meet. The self I presented to my wife this morning (the I-Celia) is a somewhat different self than the one I presented to my colleague this afternoon (the I-Irvin). At times, one's selves can compete and the individual might have to struggle to integrate these competing selves. The self a young person presents to her friends may be a different self than the one she presents to her teachers. If her friends want her to cut a class, for instance, one of these selves may be diminished.

It would appear that these selves may change, may expand and contract, may appear, disappear, and reappear over the course of our lives. Our selves are socially constructed. George Herbert Mead (1934), speaking of Helen Keller, suggested that it was not until Helen could communicate with other people "through symbols" that she could "get. . .a self" (p. 149). Berger and Luckmann (1967) maintain that human "self-production" is always and necessarily "a social enterprise." Ivan Illich and Barry Sanders (1988) see the self as "an alphabetic construct" like "word and memory, thought and history, lie and narration." They cite Benjamin Franklin's *Autobiography* as an example of self-production in its tale of Poor Richard's rise "through an encyclopedic and disparate series of selves, to. . .the Great Doctor Franklin" (p. 78).

In self-production we are all initially Poor Richards. I suggest that in adolescence we are trying to integrate our emerging selves into a totality or a single identity. In this context, Erikson (1963) might agree that the primary self that the adolescent strives to develop is the "self-as-my-work." Erikson believes that an occupational or career identity is central in adolescence. I am a future doctor, lawyer, teacher, nurse, electrician, etc. The different selves that the adolescent tries to integrate, we have seen, may or may not generate tensions. What we might call a family self, for example, might be in conflict with a peer self over an adolescent's behavior.

In an earlier book (Farrell, 1990), based on the data from a study of at-risk adolescents in New York City, I suggested a number of possible selves that the subjects of that study were dealing with: self-as-my-work, self-in-family, sexual self, self-as-loyal-friend, self-in-peer-group, self-as-student, and, for some, self-as-parent. I further suggested that those students had a difficult time integrating their selves into an identity due to family-peer, peer-school, or any other configuration of tensions. Because of the data of the current study, I suggest a somewhat different list: career self, sexual self, self-among-peers, family self, student self, and affiliating self.

Career Self

Erikson (1963) believes that the adolescent has to deal with a physiological revolution inside of him and "tangible adult tasks" ahead of him. He seeks to connect "the roles and skills cultivated earlier with the occupational prototypes of the day" (p. 261). Of course, the occupational prototype or career that the college-bound student connects with may change several times during her higher educational experience but we will see that most of the respondents in this study do indeed have such a prototype, unlike the at-risk students in my previous study (Farrell, 1990).

Sexual Self

The emergence of the sexual self is what makes adolescence different from childhood. It is, of course, a function of the physiological revolution referred to by Erikson. A number of political voices on the current scene seem to want to ignore, if not deny, that such a self exists. "Better" students are sexually restrained. Sexual abstinence is preferred as birth control and, to the most extreme voices, sex education is dangerous. The reality constructed from the students in this book, however, is that sexual activity is independent of academic achievement, gender, social class, race, or ethnic group. Sexual attitudes, however, are voiced differently by these respondents as opposed to those in the at-risk study.

Self-among-Peers

The importance of the peer group to adolescents has been researched and discussed by a myriad of educators and social scientists. Indeed, it is the existence of peer networks that has made the collection of data for this book possible. For some adolescents peer group values can come into opposition with family and societal values. For others, peers can be a source of knowledge, support, and security. What distinguishes the respondents of this study from others are their realizations about peers: they can choose their peer groups; some peer pressures must be resisted; peer groups are transitory.

Family Self

The family a person is born into is usually her primary social group, at least until adolescence. For the urban adolescents of these studies, families can be nuclear, single-parent, or extended. Their families can be their most effective support systems or their major sources of tension. The values of the family might mirror the values of society but might be opposed to the values of peer groups. Unlike the at-risk students in the previous study, virtually all of whom reported some friction with their parents, most of our respondents spoke positively about family relationships.

Student Self

What appeared to be the primary self of the respondents in this study was the student self. This, of course, is what educators believe should be the primary self. Success for the adolescent, in adult eyes, is often measured by how well he does in school. For many high school students, however, academic success is elusive and they refuse to measure their worth in such terms. For others, school becomes a source of pressure and lack of success in that endeavor causes them great distress. Some link success in school to future career success; others do not. Being able to integrate the student and career selves seems to be an important factor in achieving academic success.

The Affiliating Self

Beyond school, beyond the peer group, and beyond the family are social groups that help provide access to the greater society. What is notable about our respondents is their involvement with extracurricular and organized extraschool activities, especially as compared to at-risk students. The former hear voices from many different sources—family, pastors, teachers in nonteaching roles, youth workers, and, most of all, peers, but peers who listen to and believe the same voices.

A striking part of the data of this study is how many of our respondents attend church. For many there is a spiritual self as well as the others listed which, for a few, can become the dominant self. In the study of at-risk students, respondents were generally non-religious. Although a few were made to go to church, I saw no evidence of the development of a spiritual self in them. The at-risk students, according to the previous study's data, often hear voices exclusively of their peers; from parents and teachers they only get what they call "the speech" which they reject. I have elsewhere suggested that the lack of ability to join and form social networks might be a crucial determinant of low achievement, both economic and educational.

LISTENING TO STUDENT VOICES

Given our theoretical framework, then, how do we find out what is *in* these students that accounts for their success? Are they more able to integrate their various selves into an identity? Are the selves within each individual in conflict with each other? These questions must be answered, I think, in their own voices. To understand what is *in* them, we must try to describe their realities from their points of view. A cultural psychology, Bruner (1990) tells us, cannot dismiss what people say about their mental states and self "can only be revealed in a transaction between a teller and a told" (p. 125).

This presents some difficulties. As in my past studies, I am committed to take a collaborative and interpretive approach to ethnographic investigation and to use conversational discourse to evoke in text what Stephen Tyler (1986) calls a "possible world of commonsense reality" (p. 125) that gives a picture of the lives of successful high school students in the New York City public schools. I attempt to construct or adapt theory that answers questions like, "What accounts for student success?" and "How do the lives of these students differ from those of the less successful, previously studied, students?" Moreover, as stated above, I attempt to answer these questions in an interpretive mode or from what Frederick Erickson (1986) calls "the actors' points of view" (p. 119).

These points of view must be gathered in contexts in which students feel free to express their own ideas, their own experience, their own lore. Iona and Peter Opie (1959), in their pioneering investigations of the world of the child, point out that "[t]he scraps of lore which children learn from each other are at once more real, more immediate, more serviceable, and more vastly entertaining to them than anything which they learn from grownups" (p. 1). This, I suggest, is also true of adolescents and, for this reason, the data for this study were gathered by and from high school students.

With the help of high school teachers who were my research assistants, five high school students, who they deemed to be successful in school, were recruited to collect tape-recorded interviews between themselves and other people of their age on what their lives were like and what accounted for school success. The "interviews" were unstructured and took the form of dialogues rather than information-seeking devices. The students generated sixty-two such dialogues; the dialogues were professionally transcribed; the transcribed data were reduced with the help of the students. These data, along with the additional data from two additional separate studies collected 1) from parents and 2) from teachers, form the basis for this book. In addition, some of the data from my previous study of at-risk students were used as a basis for comparison. Both the students of the earlier study and those of this study came from the same social environments. The theme of the analysis was what makes some students succeed while others fail. The data categories, based on the theoretical framework outlined above, determined the chapters of the book. For a detailed description and discussion of the research methodology, please see the Appendix.

PLAN OF THE BOOK

Chapter 1, "The Career Self," will explore what the students in this study perceive to be the relationship between success in school and success in future life. Their career and higher educational aspirations will be surveyed. To what extent they are driven by fears of failing both in school and in later life will be investigated as well. Additionally, their hopes and aspirations on careers will be compared with those of the at-risk students previously studied.

Chapter 2, "The Sexual Self," looks at how students view boy-girl relationships. Their attitudes on contraception and responsibility to their partners will be examined. Whether they are sexually active or not and their views on sexual morality will also be discussed. This activity and their reflections on it will be compared with that of at-risk students. We will see that they have very negative attitudes toward homosexuality. Additionally, we will hear them tell where sex fits into their lives vis-à-vis school.

Chapter 3, "The Peer Self," will discuss the realization of these students that they are able to choose which of their peers will be their friends. Friends can be helpful and very important parts of one's life. On the other hand, friends can be bad influences and even dangerous. Cutting class with friends can be addictive, according to one student. That successful male students are often called nerds is a subject of concern. The pressures that students feel because of this are often great and can go as far as being physical. Successful struggles against such pressure will be described.

Chapter 4, "The Family Self," explores the nature of family interactions among this population in both nuclear and single-parent families. How they get along with their families will be compared to how students with less academic success do. Most of these students see their families as generally supportive. At-risk students reported family friction. We will look at the closeness that develops between some daughters and their mothers in single-parent families. The chapter will conclude by trying to explain how the family self is integrated with the other selves.

With separate data from a companion study, chapter 5, "Interlude—The Voices of Parents," will attempt to give a picture of the lives of parents, from their points of view and ask if student success is based on the ability of parents to pass on values to their children. Interviews conducted by parents with parents will be the basis of this chapter. We will see that the major anxiety of parents is for the safety of their children. We will examine their criticism of society and schools.

Chapter 6, "The Student Self," explores what seems to be the primary self for these students as opposed to their less academically successful peers. We will see that there is a range of achievement as well as attitudes among these students. We will also examine what gratification they are willing to forego for success in school. We will see that, although they realize the importance of school, many of them are also critical of it. However, they are do not seem to be educational reformers. We will describe their actual expectations of their schools and their teachers.

Another look into alternative data is the basis for chapter 7, "Interlude—The Voices of Teachers." What is the impact of the teacher on student success? A separate study as large as the current one, based on interviews among teachers by teachers, gives a portrait of teachers operating under very stressful circumstances. We will examine teacher attitudes toward the power structure, their students, their colleagues, the parents, and themselves. Their views of parents will be contrasted to the parents' views of them. Finally, the phenomenon of teacher burnout will be discussed.

Chapter 8, "The Affiliating Self," is an exploration into the various groups students belong to and the voices they hear because of their affiliations. Whether nonschool and nonparent voices in after-school programs, youth groups, or churches affect them as much as their families, friends, and teachers do will be examined. The influence of religion, conspicuously absent from the at-risk students in the previous study, will be investigated. We will inquire as to whether some students have developed a "spiritual self" which can help them succeed or integrate other selves.

Chapter 9, "Will—A Student Theory of Success," suggests reasons why these students succeed—but from their point of view. It examines whether there are constellations of factors that account for success rather than a single factor. The chapter discusses whether "intelligence" is crucial to success. I will suggest that a concept of "will" is what students primarily attribute their success to, although this may be embedded as well as directly stated in the data. We will look at Lev Vygotsky's (1987) theory of will for our definition of the concept. I will try to show how the internalization of the voices students hear contributes to the development of will.

Chapter 10, "Voices, Selves, and Symbolic Universes," is a theoretical chapter that analyzes how selves are created, what voices students internalize, and the social construction of meaning in the school. Do teachers' meanings of school coincide or conflict with those of students? I address whether there is an overlap in the meaning systems or what Berger and Luckmann (1967) call "symbolic universes." Do the symbolic universes of successful students contain what Carol Gilligan (1982) calls a "different voice"? Obviously, if we can communicate, there is an overlap in symbolic universes but whether there is an overlap big enough to teach and learn in for all students is problematical.

Chapter 11, "Small is Better," suggests ways of teaching, ways of creating programs and schools, ways of reorganizing existing schools to set up educational environments that would best serve students in the task of integrating their various selves. Based on the words of the students and the analysis of those words, I will suggest that the current large comprehensive high school is not the best way of educating most inner-city adolescents. I will describe a model program on the elementary level and one on the secondary level.

I would like to add that since this book is data-based, I try to maintain a researcher's objectivity without imposing my perceptions and theories to the exclusion of these young people's. Such a book should present a clear and unbiased picture of what the lives of these students are like. Not having interviewed the respondents of this study directly, I feel I can step back and look at the data with "a cold eye," to use the words of William Butler Yeats. But I was a high school teacher for many years and I cannot help injecting my own autobiographically based comments where I think it appropriate: to attempt, in Paul Ricouer's words, "[t]o understand oneself in front of a text" (1981, p. 178). Reading the textualized voices of these students created a hermeneutical circle which gave me a sense of optimism that my previous studies did not. And so, I frame these voices in the best materials available to me. Having these students in our classes would make us all better teachers.

1
The Career Self

Interviewer: So what makes you want to do well in school?

Sharon: What makes me...?

Interviewer: Want to do well in school.

Sharon: Do good in school? Um, as a lower class than other people?

Interviewer: Yeah, what I'm sayin is, what I'm tryin' to say is why do some people that's lower class, why do some turn out successful and some turn out to be garbage? Why are some drug dealers and some are just?

Sharon: All right, okay, where I live you got those two kinds of people. Now, um, okay, let's say you've got the bad and you've got the good. The bad is going nowhere. They're going straight to hell anyway, so I basically, I do that so that when I get older I won't have to live in the conditions I'm living in now. So if I just get good grades in school now and I study, I make myself. I can get good grades in college and stuff and, um, get a good job.

Interviewer: Yeah, right.

Sharon: And better myself so that I won't have to live in these conditions for the rest of my life.

Sharon's response was to a question that was asked in every interview. Every one of the students in our sample expressed the belief that there was a definite link between school and career and, furthermore, the prospect of future success was a driving force for success in school. Advanced technolgical societies such as ours, Jerome Kagan (1984) points out, need only one-third of their young people to fill the high-level skill careers that provide safety, health, economic well-being, and legal protection to others. These careers have both high pay and status and, as a result, there are more young people available than there are these desired careers. Young people must therefore be in the top third of their age cohort to qualify. Regardless of their abilities, it is difficult for minority youths in the inner-city to be recognized as being in the top third of their age cohort. Therefore, inner-city students have additional forces acting on them that have to do with their awareness of their social status and living conditions.

9

AN AGE OF DESPERATION?

What are the conditions that Sharon talks about? Is she aware of the demographic data that surfaces only from time to time in the news media? Does she know that the median income for black families in 1989 was below the comparable figure for 1969, after adjusting for inflation (O'Hare, Pollard, Mann, and Kent, 1991)? Does she know that, from 1970 to 1984, New York City lost 492,000 jobs that required less than a high school education and gained 239,000 jobs in which the average employee had some college (Wilson, 1987)? Perhaps not, but all inner-city high students see the results of these trends every day in the streets. Large numbers of homeless people seem to be everywhere, begging on the streets and many of them appear to be under thirty years old. Homelessness is the most visible social problem in our cities. To the same question that was asked of Sharon about what makes her do well in school, Peter had, perhaps, a more graphic but not a dissimilar response.

> Peter: Well, sometimes in myself I just...it's just a...it's not really a desperate desire to achieve, but rather a fear of failing, you know, fear of being a bum or something like that. After seeing what people have to go through to get a meal, what some people have to go through to get money...you know, the type of job some people have to get because they're uneducated or something like that. You know that really propels me to keep doing what I'm doing.

But, of course, it *is* a desperate desire to succeed. Developing a career self can become a desperate search for many young people. Peter's response is reminicent of that of a young man in my study of at-risk students (Farrell, 1990). The young man did not have a history of school success and was in a dropout prevention program while looking for a job.

> Cuz you know the thing that scares me the most is fuckin' havin' no future. That really scares me....One of my greatest fears is gowin' up and bein' a bum....Cuz you know them niggers look sorry as shit....Sometimes I be lookin' at them...and I be like damn, that might be me in twenty five years, man...How the fuck can you be happy with no money? You have to beg niggers for fifty cents. Damn, what the fuck is this? (p. 14)

That both groups of students voice the same fears is remarkable. Growing up in New York, it never occurred to me that I might end up on the streets. Few of the readers of this book have ever felt that kind of fear. Youth should be a time of fearlessness and hope for the future. Erik Erikson speaks of American youth as "proud of its independence and burning with initiative" (1963, p. 323). The age where one develops a career self and tries to integrate it into an identity should not be an age of desperation. We might expect varying degrees of adolescent rebellion but not, in a century characterized by a rising standard of living in this country, fears of becoming a homeless beggar.

Do most young people really worry about this? White mainstream America has generally seen and presented adolescents as likeable and earnest people with few worries about future careers. In the late 1930s, the commercially successfull Andy Hardy movie character, admirably played by Mickey Rooney in the series of eight films, was always more worried about the new girl in town than in his future even though he was growing up in the Great Depression. After World War II and through the 1950s, the archtypical adolescent was the radio and comic strip character, Archie Andrews, who could have been called "Son of Andy Hardy." The hippies of the 1960s made us uncomfortable because they often chose to be homeless beggars—though most had the option of going home when things got tough—but stereotypes of them were assimilated into Broadway musicals, again as likeable and earnest people little bothered by finding jobs, much less careers.

Vietnam erected a wall between many adolescents and their future careers. Young people of the 1970s were presented in the entertainment media as likeable and earnest people living in pre-Vietnam times. The TV series "Happy Days" and the widely hailed films *American Graffiti* and *American Hot Wax* succeeded because of the goodheartedness of the characters—even those with leather jackets—still struggling with Andy Hardy's problems with the added burden, perhaps, of the death of the rock 'n roll singer, Buddy Holly. In the 1980s, the actor, Michael J. Fox, became prominent playing a career-oriented young man but was reduced to a comic caricature of a budding Yuppie who always finds out, in the end, that family is more important than his future as an investment banker. Ever responsive to markets, situation comedies on TV now give us pictures of black adolescents, always comic, always likeable and earnest, never having feelings of desperation.

This picture was jarred for many Americans by evening news clips of young people during the Los Angeles looting in the late spring of 1992. But most of the audience, I suggest, preferred to see the looters as criminal opportunists rather than desperate people. For it is easy to understand how adolescents in the poorest of Third World countries, in countries destroyed by civil war, in countries stifled by political and cultural repression, become desperate men and women. They may be driven to become revolutionaries, criminals, or beggars. They may take enormous risks like crossing seas in small boats or sneaking across borders. They may live their days in life-or-death situations. But inner-city students can also be in life-and-death situations. Your chances of being murdered in Detroit are greater than those in Belfast, Northern Ireland. And the slower deaths of street beggars and drug addicts who come out of your neighborhoods and who are the same color as you present a terrifying spectre.

Barbel Inhelder and Jean Piaget (1958), in *The Growth of Logical Thinking from Childhood to Adolescence*, the major influence on the study of cognitive development in adolescence, see the acquisition of a future orientation as the underlying change between that period and what has gone before. After presenting their detailed analysis of data collected over years, they write:

On a naive global level, without trying to distinguish between the student, the apprentice, the young worker, or the young peasant in terms of how their social attitudes may vary, the adolescent differs from the child *above all* in that he thinks beyond the present. The adolescent is the individual who commits himself to possibilities—although we certainly do not mean to deny that his commitment begins in real life situations. (p. 339, emphasis added)

In spite of Andy Hardy, the future is paramount for the adolescent and, in the inner city, the prospect of a career is the only long-term balm for the desperation he is likely to feel. It is the major justification for delayed rather than the immediate gratification of peer socializing, cutting classes, experimenting with drugs, or worse. For middle-class high school students, only the vaguest notions of what they will do in life are necessary. They know there are "tangible adult tasks," to use Erikson's words, that they can choose later. Working-class high school students in the days when the United States relied on an industrial rather than a service economy also knew there were "tangible adult tasks" to be performed and for which they might be rewarded. The students interviewed here seemed to speak of only the highly visible career tasks. Bill Cosby's character on his recent popular TV show is an obstetrician-gynecologist married to a lawyer.

In virtually all interviews, students were asked what they wanted as a future occupation. In most cases, the respondents had already decided. The vast majority of those who did, chose professions and, of these, medicine was the first choice. Both young men and young women spoke of being obstetricians, pediatricians, and gynecologists. Other careers mentioned were journalism, electrical engineering, architecture, computers, business. One, we will see below, planned on going into his father's business but was going to college first and only one did not plan to attend college. He thought he would do something having to do with electricity. It was rare to find a prospective tradesman. The choices of these young people bear out the views of Kagan (1984), cited above, on the high-status, highly paid, highly skilled careers.

RACISM, EDUCATION, AND THE JOB CEILING

Race, unfortunately, for many Americans distinguishes these young people from those in the majority culture. John Ogbu (1978, 1989) explained this when he differentiated among minority groups and introduced the concept of the "job ceiling." Obgu developed a typology that distinguished the quality of majority-minority relations. As Foley (1991) points out, not all of America's minorities might fit into Ogbu's typology but the construct still has value for us in this analysis to show the added stresses that our respondents have to carry in their quests for success.

Ogbu writes of "autonomous," "immigrant," and "caste" minorities. The first have a definite cultural identity and choose to maintain that identity (e.g., Hasidic Jews); the second have chosen to come to a new country; caste minorities, however, are politically, economically, and culturally subordinated to the majority group by virtue of birth. The Maoris of New Zealand, the Burakumin of Japan, untouchables in India, and African-Americans are examples of caste minorities. Caste minorities, according to Ogbu, are hampered in occupational choice by the "job ceiling." This operates by restricting caste members in competing freely on the job market; they are not permitted to obtain their proportionate share of the most desirable jobs.

How does the job ceiling, we ask, affect the motivations of minority adolescents to achieve both in the workforce and in school? Early in his career, Robert LeVine (1967) suggested that achievement motivation might not be strongly linked to socialization practices; children may come to realize on their own what their chances for social mobility are. Moreover, LeVine said, these realizations are likely to be accurate. Twenty-five years later, Sharon, whose remarks began this chapter, seems to understand the problems of social mobility, even though she probably does not have much access to accurate demographic data. Neither she nor most other respondents come from middle-class homes, homes where the possibility of downward mobility is never even considered. She is confronted daily with such a prospect.

Does what Sharon knows intuitively affect her choice of career or her performance in school? Might not even the hint of the existence of a job ceiling act to discourage a student's achievement and aspirations? Ogbu (1978) maintains that neither the schools nor the homes of caste minority children, in this or other countries, adequately prepare them to successfully compete with members of the dominant group. What then makes the young people in our sample achieve and maintain such high aspirations? And why do others fail to achieve?

I would argue that the knowledge or intuition of the job ceiling is precisely what makes them want to join the ranks of professionals. That so many of them aspire to become credentialed professionals points to a belief, correct in my opinion, that the job ceiling is less constraining in these environments. While there are still relatively few black men in professional and managerial occupations their numbers, according to the Bureau of Labor Statistics (O'Hare et al., 1991), have risen from 4 percent in 1949 to 13 percent in 1990. And while it would be naive to say there is no job ceiling in the professions, a physician or a Ph.D. is more apt to be judged on his credentials and ability than his caste status. Advanced degrees cannot be taken away and few holders of such expect to be on unemployment lines.

Now it is obvious that not all these students will achieve what they set out to do. There are many more premed majors among college freshmen than among college seniors. A person who gets a C in comparative anatomy may wisely change her major to English. (This is not to demean English; it was my major.) But they are still in the university environment and still hold to the value that education leads to success. Some may pursue business careers; others may enter teacher training or various levels of government service, both of which are less restrictive and more accommodating to minorities. Specific aspirations may change but as long as young people have access to environments that promote upward mobility—like higher education—they need not be crushed.

I will argue below and in chapter 6 that, although the future is paramount to adolescents, they do not all see a *direct* link between what they are studying (e.g., algebra and French) and future success even though they believe that it would be good to complete school. Also in chapter 9, I will suggest that a history of a lack of success in school discourages many young people from expending further effort and may lead them to disparage education. This was certainly true of many of the at-risk students in my previous study (Farrell, 1990).

Ceilings in Other Cultures

Cross cultural studies support these conclusions. Ogbu (1978, 1989), after analyzing a wide variety of field studies both by individual researchers and government agencies in Great Britain, concludes that the job ceiling does, in fact, exist for second and third generation West Indians. He cites a number of researchers (Braithwaite, 1968; Bowker, 1968; Rose, 1969; Gibson, 1988) who suggest that this ceiling has a definite influence on school performance of West Indians and other minorities. Ogbu finds many similarities between West Indians in Britain and African-Americans regarding the job ceiling and education. He saw West Indians as originally being eager to be assimilated into British society but cites Rose (1969) as suggesting that many "withdraw" into such social groups as the Pentecostal church movement or into "cultural nationalism in the context of negritude" (p. 439).

The Maoris in New Zealand, according to Ogbu, are also hampered by a job ceiling. As a group, they are less educated than the dominant white culture and those of them who are educated tend to be civil servants. African-Americans, as stated above, are also drawn to government jobs. The plurality of jobs in the inner city of New York are with city or state agencies. There is a weekly newspaper called *The Chief* which is completely devoted to civil service job listings, information, and test dates. To some it is the most important paper in the city. Like African-Americans, Maoris are underrepresented in the professions. Differences in employment opportunities for Maoris are not, according to Ogbu, overcome by education. In addition, writes Ogbu, teacher expectations, and biased textbooks and curriculums contribute to lower Maori school performance. Critics of American education maintain that these factors exist in our schools as well.

In India, the country most identified with a caste system—even though it has been legally eradicated—the lower castes are attracted to education because, according to Ogbu, it allows them to improve their statuses as individuals, if not as a group; the job ceiling is in effect. Like African-Americans, especially those in cities, they are drawn to the civil service. Education can enable them to enter what Ogbu calls "the technoeconomic system of modern India" (p. 299). He cites Beteille (1967) as suggesting that the lower castes most often refuse to enter craft training schools out of a preference for professional and white-collar jobs. One wonders if there are similar phenomena operating when so few of our respondents express an interest in skilled trades which, in New York City, are highly paid.

The Optimists

Not all students expressed desperation, of course. The future professionals seemed very upbeat. But I suggest that those who mentioned careers in medicine are probably not aware of the particular demands of that profession. They have an image of a doctor but might not know specifically what a doctor does. They well might change their minds later but, for now, the image of a future career sustains them. A few students, however, are willing to defer specific choices till later. Like James, they are willing to tolerate uncertainty.

> Interviewer: What do you plan to do after high school? This is your last year, right?
> James: Yes, I'm planning to go to college. Either Fordham, Pace, Stony Brook [State University], or maybe Baruch [City University]. I plan to study business, business administration. I'm not really sure yet which school I'll be accepted to so, you know, I'll just have to see and see if my grades get me in.
> Interviewer: Is there anything specifically you want to do?
> James: Well, I'm really not sure. I want to study business, but ever since I was a kid I always liked the cops.

James is confident, optimistic, and realistic. He was the only student who expressed an interest in being a policeman and, in fact, in any civil service job. That is understandable in that policing is such a visible profession; few people know what most other civil servants do. James, incidentally, is in a selective business-oriented program in his high school. And he may not have made his final decision but he holds on to what will enable him to do so—education.

Cathy and Roberta seem to echo Erikson's view of youth as independent and full of initiative.

> Interviewer: What are some of the expectations that you have for yourself?
> Cathy: I want to. . .I don't know what profession I want to be in like in between, but whatever I choose to do I wish to succeed and to have a family and to be the best that I can be.

Roberta, below, feels that the world is her oyster. But she has a wide range of possibilities, from stardom to the practical. Adults may chuckle at this range but also admire her belief that anything is possible.

> Roberta: There are so many things. I want to be a singer or a teacher, a stewardess, psychologist.

Pedro, however, the young man referred to above who expected to go into his father's business, is not typical among this group. That his father has his own business gives the son a great sense of security.

> Pedro: Let's see, I want to do well in school. But you know, I apply myself in high school and go to a good college and, um, you know, take control of my father's business. And then, um, you know, I mean if I have to, I'll get married.

A higher proportion of Hispanics own businesses than African-Americans but a lower proportion of them attend college, according to the National Center for Education Statistics (1990). Data from the Bureau of the Census indicate that African-Americans own 3 percent of America's firms but those firms account for 1 percent of business income (O'Hare et al., 1991). In surburban, small-town, and rural high schools there are always some number of students who will follow in their father's footsteps. Statistically, few of our respondents, however, have this option open to them.

SCHOOL AND CAREERS

That these students have definite career aspirations is probably both a cause and an effect of their school success. Even if they later change their minds, their views of the future give them a direction that they can verbalize and be reinforced for. Where, one asks, did they get these directions? In chapter 4, we will see that their families encourage and sometimes pressure them to succeed in school but there were no indications that families pushed them toward specific occupations. Guidance counselors, because of their enormous caseloads, give very little career guidance as we will see in chapter 10. Nor is there any evidence that they get their career selves from their friends. These students, we will see in chapter 3, have come to realize that they pick their peers. There is no instance in these dialogues of two friends having the same career expectations. It would seem that they get their ideas and make these choices independently.

Special Programs

New York has a number of elite high schools that, in my opinion, provide as good an education as do any of the famous prep schools in this country. The students in this study were *not* drawn from those schools; we need to know how students function in mainstream district schools. However, there are a number of "magnet" schools (institutions devoted to a particular theme: humanities, science, or a specific career area) in the system and many theme programs within mainstream schools. A few of the respondents were in these theme programs. There are also alternative schools in the city system, which will be discussed in the last chapter, and vocational schools, some excellent like the School for Fashion Industries, which prepare students for a range of careers. Others, however, are dumping grounds for less successful students.

Do these schools contribute to a student's career choice? For some, the answer is yes. These schools and programs might be brought to the attention of successful elementary and junior high school students by teachers, administrators, and guidance counselors but this often seems to happen only by chance. If a student is absent the day a particular announcement is made about admission to such programs she may lose out. As was said before, there is relatively little organized career guidance given in schools covering the whole spectrum of careers; students do not see the variety of tangible adult tasks that exist.

There seems to be little attention given to careers in areas other than the professions. While I was teaching a graduate course for teachers in a public high school in the Bronx, I learned that the woodshop had been closed as a cost-saving measure. A bright young man I know in another state who dropped out of high school has always been able to support himself because of his knowledge of hand tools which he gained in a high school shop. He would not be called highly skilled but he can get a job as a framing carpenter or, more likely in the present economy, in maintainance. In New York City, apartment and office maintainance pays a living, if not a princely, wage. Skilled craftsmen, as I have said, do well, especially if they have skills that can be transferred across fields.

At the risk of sounding like the junior high school teacher in *The Autobiography of Malcolm X* who, because of the "realities" of the race situation, advised Malcolm to become a carpenter when the young man expressed an interest in being a lawyer, I would suggest that not everyone can be a doctor or a lawyer. We should, of course, like Emerson, encourage all our young people to hitch their wagons to the stars but we should also show them the range of career possibilities and give them the wherewithal to make some basic decisions. They should know that you can't fix a Toyota unless you have a set of metric sprocket wrenches or that too heavy a hammer will bend too thin a nail. A former professor of vocational education bragged to a group I was in that his department no longer did vocational education; they did technology. They are no longer training teachers to show our young people how to hammer nails, replace carburetors, or to plumb a house. But who, I would ask, will teach them to change faucet washers?

Teachers

Are individual teachers a source of career guidance? Other than parents, the teacher is the most often seen representative of the world of work. Yet teachers, at least high school teachers, we will see in chapter 6, are perceived by students as being almost totally caught up in teaching their subject matter. And it is difficult for many students, successful as well as at-risk, to see how conjugating French verbs and the like will contribute to their future careers. It is difficult for teachers to show them such connections as well. Our respondents apparently see a general connection between school and career success but they do not seem to be guided to specific careers by teachers. For many students, the connection between school and career is too vague.

The majority of the teachers of our respondents are white and of the dominant culture. Seeing the connection between school and career means buying into the dominant culture. But knowing, on some level, of phenomena like job ceilings might make young people wary of doing this. That only one expressed an interest in being a teacher must say something of how these young people perceive their own teachers. I suggest that seeing more minority teachers—even if these young people do not choose to become part of that profession—will make them less wary of the dominant culture. They need to see people like them who are successful because they have bought into and can recreate American culture. They need to be shown by people they trust that there is a connection between school and career.

The Subject Matter of School

If these young people are not, for whatever the reason, in special programs and if their teachers are not helping them develop career selves, who or what contributes to self construction? Are they able to make independent judgments based on what they learn in school? Do they experiment in a chemistry or biology lab, read a book like *The Double Helix*, and decide to embark on a career to code the DNA molecule? Do they read the poems of Dylan Thomas or the novels of Richard Wright and decide they want to write a great novel on love and death? Do they become immersed in the computer culture and decide they want to develop computers receptive to the human voice? Do they come to love the smell of wood and decide to fashion objects that have never been made before? I do not know. We will see in chapter 6 that they rarely talk about the content of their courses.

But I was a secondary school teacher for twenty years and I have to believe that my students grappled with ideas, thrilled to the poetry, and incorporated some of material I taught into their lives. I also have to believe that the students in this study see some rewards other than good grades for their academic endeavors. Perhaps the more basic rewards of school endeavor drive them. Getting a correct answer on an algebra word problem may give someone a small sense of triumph. Having similar small triumphs every day might have helped these students trust that they themselves will find a place in the technological world in which they live.

THE GOOD-, THE BAD-, AND THE NOT-ME

We have seen that school and career are interlinked among these young people. The search for a career drives them but we ask whether they are living their lives in the manner of typical American adolescents, like all "good kids," or whether racism in the form of a job ceiling makes theirs a desperate quest. In other words, how deeply are they affected by their environment? To answer this we might look to how Harry Stack Sullivan (1953), whose work is one of the theoretical underpinnings of this book, elaborated on his theory of the self system; he speculated on how that system develops through the life span. Sullivan pointed to a number of what he referred to as personifications within the self that are created in interpersonal relations as we grow up. He suggested that there were three personifications of the self—the *good-me*, the *bad-me*, and the *not-me*.

According to Sullivan, humans are exposed to these three personifications before the end of infancy; they are part of the socialization process. They are phases of what will be part of *me*. In every instance of a child being trained for life in whatever culture, said Sullivan, there will be these three personifications. The *good-me* is the beginning personification which organizes experience. In this respect, it is like the Freudian *ego*. It is what most people mean when they use the word "I." This personification is introduced by what Sullivan calls "the mothering person" and is further constructed and reconstructed in all the developing human's interpersonal relations. The good-me is introduced by the family and is further developed in relations with peers and with school personnel.

The *bad-me* begins to be developed when anxiety comes to be associated with behavior. Anxiety has its beginning form in *others* who induce the anxiety. Like the good-me, the bad-me begins very early in life and continues to be formed in those interpersonal relationships that result in anxiety. A teacher or a parent may be seen by a student as sitting in judgment on her when the student's anxiety is increased after she gets back a paper full of red-penciled corrections coupled with a poor grade. This anxiety contributes to the bad-me, the part of me that others do not like. This is the part of me that fails tests, cuts classes, or ignores assignments. It is difficult not to have a bad-me develop in school.

Sullivan saw, as a characteristic of late adolescence, that some young people become "extremely agile" at discerning the smallest hint of anxiety and avoiding the situation. Even in the best of schools, when young people are making life decisions based very much on their school performance, there is bound to be anxiety. The bad-me will not get into college; why should I then take difficult courses? Less successful students might have developed more of a bad-me than successful ones. Sullivan maintained that anxiety must be tolerated and in an "educative experience" the young person must deal with its source. He writes:

> The problem of the psychiatrist [read, teacher] is more or less to spread a larger context before the patient [read student]; insofar as that succeeds, the [student] realizes that, anxiety or not, the present way of life is unsatisfactory and is unprofitable in the sense that it is not changing things for the better; whereupon, in spite of anxiety, other things being equal, the self-system can be modified.

The respondents in this study apparently can see the larger context. They make a connection between school and career success which enables them to tolerate the anxiety that school necessarily brings. But there is an additional personification which, for them, may act as an incentive in that it is something to avoid but, for their less academically successful peers, acts as a source of terror. Peter, in the second section of this chapter, spoke of his desire to succeed as emanating from his fear of being a bum. And the virtually identical fear was voiced in the same section by the student in the dropout prevention program. To reiterate, the specter of homeless men and women, not ten years older than they are, ragged and begging on the street and the perceived possibility that they could become like these people may well be terrifying. This specter is a living vision of the *not-me*.

The not-me is encountered mostly, according to Sullivan, in dreams and nightmares. The not-me comes from poorly grasped aspects of life, incidents of intense anxiety, which are later associated with "awe, horror, loathing, or dread." The good-me and the bad-me are part of conscious experience as opposed to the not-me. Under exceptional circumstances, says Sullivan, we have an awareness of the not-me. I suggest that the ubiquitous presence of homeless men or women which even the most secure of us find appalling raises the specter of the not-me in the consciousness of these young people. The vast majority of the homeless in the cities are people of color and, while there have always been panhandlers in the cities, the current numbers are unprecedented in my lifetime. The homeless person is not me and my emotions about him run from pity to annoyance to loathing. But if I were to perceive him, on some level, as *my* not-me-who-might-become-me, a very real terror might be added to what I feel. The homeless beggar can become one of a young person's "possible" selves (Markus and Nurius, 1986; Gergen, 1967, 1972), as we will see in chapter 10. The effects on young people of the daily sight of large numbers of those, young and old, who have failed at life cannot be exaggerated.

These respondents offer the good-me when they use the word "I." They tolerate the anxiety of having others judge the bad-me. They are driven, consciously and unconsciously, by fleeing the terror of the not-me. These three personifications of the self are intertwined with their futures and they need to see their futures in terms of careers. Their less successful peers must also be driven by the terror of the not-me but may not be as willing to tolerate the anxiety of being judged the bad-me and may simply avoid these judgmental experiences. Shawn voices the power of the good-me which has become his "I" in spite of many serious obstacles.

> Shawn: I've got a lot of problems. I've got a lot of problems that I have to deal with every day, mostly my health, my family, and other things that go on every day. But I consider my school work very important and I want to make something of myself, even if I'm not alive to enjoy it.

A good kid, a desperate kid, or both?

2
The Sexual Self

The young people in this study spoke to a variety of sexual activity and attitudes. One of our interviewers, at one point or another in the dialogues she initiated, posed the same question to almost all of her respondents. The two answers which follow below were taken from two separate dialogues of hers that occurred on different days. The two interiewees were acquainted but neither was aware at the time that the other was being interviewed. Tony gave a very honest and unexpected answer for a young man.

> Interviewer: Are you still a virgin?
> Tony: No, I wish I was.
> Interviewer: Why do you say that?
> Tony: Because I wouldn't be ashamed when the subject or something comes
> up around my parents.

Cassie's response was equally unexpected but, each of the student interviewers agreed, she was honest, humorous, and her feelings were not at all atypical even if they do not reflect traditional attitudes.

> Interviewer: Are you still a virgin?
> Cassie: Damn. Unfortunately, yes. That's sad, isn't it?

THE ONSET OF SEXUAL ACTIVITY

In our culture (simply meaning the way of life in North American postindustrial society at the end of the twentieth century) with puberty comes sexuality. The sexual self which normally lies dormant in childhood manifests itself at puberty and can become the dominant self of adolescence and adulthood. Such a prospect is disturbing to many adults and often frightening to those, such as parents, clergymen, and educators, who have direct responsibility for the development of young people. There has rarely been agreement among adults as to what is the appropriate time in a young person's life when he or she, especially she, should be able to engage in various sexual practices. But since human beings reach sexual maturity as early as eleven years of age, it would be preposterous to think that they will all wait some socially defined number of years after that point before engaging in behaviors that nature does not prohibit.

The Psychology of Adolescent Sexuality

Jerome Kagan (1984) speaks to the physical, emotional, and cognitive changes that occur when one reaches adolescence. In the natural course of human development, hormonal secretions give rise to the emotion of sexual excitment. "The adolescent," he writes, "is aware of her ability to meet the local standards of sexual attraction and romantic success." Both boys and girls weigh "their sexual competence and initiate or withdraw from participation in accord with their private evaluation of the degree to which they deviate from the standard of appropriate sexual characteristics" (p. 179).

Regarding cognition and sexuality, Kagan (1984) goes on to address the implications of Piaget's (1950) theory of formal operations in which the developing human being gains the ability to analyze his belief systems for "logical consistency." Because of some of the preposterous attitudes toward sexuality, referred to above, that are held by some segments of society, the young person might be unable to discern any logical consistency between societal attitudes and his own or his peers' behavior. This results in a form of "cognitive dissonance" (p. 179), an example of which, Kagan gives in a set of three propositions.

1. Sexual activity—self administered or interpersonally experienced—is bad.
2. Sexuality provides pleasure.
3. If sex is pleasant, it should not be bad. (p. 181)

The only way to resolve the dissonance here, says Kagan, is to deny the first proposition. Such a denial, however, may well lead the adolescent to question and doubt many other societal strictures and values as well. If what they tell you about sex is wrong, perhaps what they tell you about drugs, careers, schooling, and friends could be wrong too. But our respondents, as we have seen in the last chapter about careers or will see in following chapters on the peer and student selves, do not tend to reject adult values. Tony, whose voice began this chapter, seems to have experienced guilt rather than cognitive dissonance over his sexual behavior. Psychoanalysts may want to argue that he is sexually repressed but I suggest that his family self which we will look at in chapter 4 is more dominant at this time in his life than his sexual self.

Erik Erikson in *Childhood and Society* (1963), even though he is generally seen to take a psychoanalytic perspective, suggests something else. Erikson, of course, is known for his eight-stage theory of human development. He posits that adolescence is the time in a young person's life when she searches for her "identity" and this search takes precedence over sexuality. As outlined in the introduction to this book, the adolescent is primarily interested in deciding on a *career* identity, defined as successfully connecting "the roles and skills cultivated earlier with the occupational prototypes of the day" (p. 261). Only after having solidified her identity can the young person successfully proceed to the following stages of intimacy, defined as a relationship with one other person, and then generativity, defined as guiding the next generation. Erikson goes so far as to suggest that even falling in love for adolescents is, to a considerable extent, an attempt to find one's identity by reflecting it on and off another and is *not*, therefore, primarily sexual.

The voices we heard in the last chapter would seem to support Erikson's theory that career identity is the primary concern of these young people, if not of the less academically successful young people that I encountered in my study of at-risk students (Farrell, 1990). Gilligan (1982), however, believes that Erikson is only talking of the male adolescent in his explanation of identity. She agrees with Erikson that, in the male, identity precedes intimacy and generativity but she disagrees with his later analysis (1968, after *Childhood and Society*) that the woman puts the search for her identity on hold while she attracts a man. Gilligan suggests that identity, intimacy, and generativity seem to be "fused" in a woman's development. To support Gilligan's denial that women put their identities on hold, it should be pointed out that the majority of the voices in the last chapter who were so concerned about future careers were the voices of young women.

While I cannot survey the entire range of the psychological literature on adolescent sexuality here—and even if I could I doubt that there would be a consensus—I think we can agree that adolescents are sexual beings. We do not have to be orthodox psychoanalysts to suggest that humans have sexual selves from the earliest years. The sexual self begins to manifest itself as a competing force with the other selves at puberty. To find out how dominant this self is to our respondents, we will have to listen to their voices.

Subordinating the Sexual Self

Only one of fifty-two male respondents in my study of at-risk high school students would admit to being a virgin and then only by inference. The question was not often asked by my student collaborators in that study. Either they assumed that everyone was sexually active or, I suggest, they did not wish to have to answer the question themselves. When it was asked, most of the young women in that study refused to answer and one emphatically denied it. Among the current respondents, a few of the women refused to answer but most did. The surprising results were that young women could admit to not being virgins; young men could admit that they were. I might add that the subject of sex was discussed in every dialogue and respondents were very open about it. Of course, many of the respondents were friends or, at least, previously acquainted with the interviewers. Among this group of students, there appears to be a great deal of honesty about one's sexual behavior.

An example of controlling sexual behavior, if not subordinating the sexual self, is David who lost his virginity at twelve because of peer pressure, as he explains it to his interviewer, and who states he is currently sexually active. To the question of when and under what circumstances it is all right to have sex, he had an answer which some might find surprising in view of his experience.

> David: Well, it all depends. For me, I believe you should wait. Because if you truly love that person you wouldn't.... [*inaudible*] In a lot of relations in my personal experience, what I have to say is that if I'm in a relationship with the person and...I'll wait.

I would caution that David's interviewer was a young woman and, although she believed his response to be honest, he might feel the need to say something different to a male.

But Gerald had a similar response to the same interviewer's questions on sex. Gerald is a sports-minded young man who has a girlfriend, who professes to be a Christian, and who wants to be a pediatrician.

> Interviewer: At what age did you lose your virginity?
> Gerald: Seven.
> Interviewer: What was the cause? What happened?
> Gerald: Boredom. (laughs)
> Interviewer: Why boredom? What happened?
> Gerald: In Jamiaca there's not much to do, but, you know, to watch T.V. and go outside and play around. So, you know you get curious and want to do stuff.
> Interviewer: How old was the girl?
> Gerald: Six.
> Interviewer: Are you serious?
> Gerald: Six!
> Interviewer: Okay, thank you. What are your opinions on sex before marriage?
> Gerald: Um, I don't like it too well.
> Interviewer: Excuse me?
> Gerald: I don't agree with it too well.

Gerald's interviewer appears to be quite surprised at his responses. But Gerald seems to be very thoughtful young man. He is critical of school and government, close to his family, against capital punishment. He believes in sex education and teaching young people their "responsibilites." There is no indication that he is in any way sexually repressed and is not mouthing adult platitudes. Gerald, I would say, chooses to subordinate his sexual self to his career, family, student, and religious selves. It would seem that he deals with the cognitive dissonance referred to by Kagan, above, by modifying rather than denying the first proposition: "Sexual activity. . . is bad [at certain times in one's life]." Gerald's attitudes may not be what is expected but he is a successful student who seems satisfied with his life.

Boyfriends and Girlfriends

If Gerald's attitudes are not the norm for this population, what is? What types of sexual behavior are acceptable to them? What do they value about sexuality and sexual relationships? In general, it would seem that having a boyfriend or girlfriend is valued. Among the less successful students of my previous study, none of the males mentioned having a girlfriend. Most (fifteen of twenty-one) young women in that group, however, referred of their boyfriends but did not describe them in any great detail. Some of the respondents in this study, however, tell a great deal about their significant others. Sean speaks very tenderly about his ex-girlfriend.

> Interviewer: Did your last girlfriend influence you in any kind of way?
> Sean: The person played a very important role in my life, even if she doesn't know it. I mean the person was very special. When I was going and doing things without her knowing what I was going through, she helped me a lot just by smiling and just by being there. And just by doing things that maybe she didn't think were important, but in my heart they meant something to me and they kept me going a lot and you know I don't have no regrets, even though sometimes I get upset with the person and I say things, but deep inside my heart I have no regrets and she's a very special person in my heart and I consider her my best friend now.

Other students speak of caring relationships. One young woman told of her boyfriend checking with her on whether she finished her homework. Of course, some might argue that this is a form of control rather than caring. But boyfriends or girlfriends among our respondents often serve as motivators for their partners to do well in school. The young men in our sample seemed to feel the same needs for affiliation as the young women in this regard. Approximately half the males and half the females spoke of having or having had a boyfriend or girlfriend. Most of the others spoke of wanting to have a serious relationship.

But some of these students also see a downside to relationships. Rosie complains, "Everybody knows me as Bill's girl instead of Rosie. Oh there goes Bill's girl." Jennie expresses a need for contact with boys but is not interested in having a boyfriend.

> Jennie: No, I don't have a boyfriend but I go on dates because, you know, I feel like having a boyfriend and you know, come on—these girls have boyfriends and already they get pregnant, dropping out of school, not finishing school and they're messing up and everything.

Anxiety and Pressures

These students also speak of the concerns about sexuality and relationships that one would expect all adolescents to have. They seem to be more open about their fears than students in the previous study. The males among those students seemed to want to project a sense of bravado in their dealing with the opposite sex. In the following dialogue, Ken, without bravado, speaks for many young men.

> Interviewer: If you saw a girl standing at the bus stop, would you walk up to her?
> Ken: No.
> Interviewer: Even if she was stunningly beautiful, you wouldn't?
> Ken: No, I wouldn't. Why? Simple, I'm afaid she'd dis me [verbally put him down].

The young women here, like the young women in the previous study, complained about young men pressuring them to have sex.

> Interviewer: Do you think you've ever been pressured to drink or have sex?
> Gelsie: Not to drink but to have sex with this guy. I remember we were just going out for a month. Third day we started going out, like from then on he started asking me to prove myself to him and everything like that. But after that we broke up and everything. But he was the first guy that I saw hungry. Guys are hungry.

When another interviewer says she is interested in someone, Lonny asks his name. When she hears it, it is obvious that she knows the young man for she screeches her question.

> Lonny: Have you ever been pressured into having sex with anybody?
> Interviewer: Pressured? Guys! Like baby—I hate it when guys do that. Like "Baby, I love you." And I'm, "Don't feed me that 'I love you' bullcrap. You don't love me, you just want to. . . ." I hate that.

The young men here, although sometimes willing to admit their fears did not speak of pressure to have sex. The other young men in the study of at-risk students, did. One even admitted to lying about having sex with a particular young woman because of his friends. Another spoke of his father being seventeen when he was born but that he, at seventeen, hadn't even had a girlfriend yet. He verbalized that he felt somehow left out that he hadn't gotten a girl pregnant yet. Apparently, the young men among the respondents of the current study are not as driven by peer pressure. Like any other adolescent, the typical young man in this population has fears and anxieties about sex but, apparently, he is able to keep them in a meaningful perpective.

It is difficult to say what percentage of these young people are or have been sexually active. Only one interviewer asked the question directly. Of her twenty-two respondents, fourteen were women with six admitting to being or having been sexually active, five not, and three refusing to answer; of the eight men, four were or had been sexually active, four not. The Children's Defense Fund (1988) maintained that 47 percent of women between the ages of fifteen and nineteen were sexually active. While I do not necessarily doubt these figures I am sceptical as to how they were determined. I have no data to suggest that the young people of the earlier study were any more or less sexually active than these. Of males, I can only say that some of these young men who abstain do so by choice, others by lack of opportunity; of the earlier group, I am led to believe that lack of opportunity is the prime explanation for abstinance. Of females in this study, both choice and lack of opportunity are working; of females in the earlier study, it was impossible to tell.

Desired Qualities

What do these young people look for as desired qualities in the opposite sex? When asked by a female interviewer what he looked for in a girl, Gary reflected for a few moments before he spoke.

> Gary: Well, . . . if they look okay, smart. Besides the body, they've got to be smart, caring, sensitive.
> Interviewer: Do you feel beauty, uh, in a girl's weight or shape depends. . . . Does it help in deciding whether to approach her or go out with her?
> Gary: No, not really but I wouldn't go out with an ugly girl. If she doesn't look that bad, I'd go and talk to her because it's not her looks, it's what's inside her.

The same interviewer asked another young man, Oscar, a similar set of questions. Although he offered one flip response in his answer, his tone was judged to be very serious by the student interviewers.

> Interviewer: If you're looking for a girl to have a relationship with, what are some of the specific characteristics—I don't mean she's cute, what is cute? I want you to describe your ideal girl or a girl that you would be interested in going out with. Not speaking only of her mind because that's bullshit but, um, what are some of the specific characteristics that you look for in a girl?
> Oscar: Honest, easy to talk to, respectable, and intellectual.
> Interviewer: Physical features, what do you look for?
> Oscar: 38-26-36.
> Interviewer: Interesting. Do you think that a person's weight or looks influences whether you're interested in them or not?
> Oscar: Yes and no. Yes, I don't want to be seen with no big, overweight girl and no, cuz it's not really how a person looks, it's her personality.

But none of the males who were asked similar questions about how their ideal should look were as specific as Kathy, below. A different female interviewer from the one above asked her what was the first thing she looked for in a prospective boyfriend.

> Kathy: The first thing? This might sound funny, but he has to have a nice body. You just see him in his jeans and he looks all firm. And lips, nice full beautiful African lips.

In general, there did not seem to be a great deal of difference in how young men answered these types of questions as opposed to young women. Nor were there any differences expressed in the importance of having relationships. The young women did not express greater affiliation needs than the young men. Young women in my previous study spoke of boyfriends more than they did of family. This was not the case with the academically successful young women. One of these, Renee, suggests that her affiliation needs could be filled by her family at this time in her life.

> Renee: I would like him to respect me, you know, to love me or like me or whatever. To be real honest with me. I wouldn't like him—if he had a lot of money—I wouldn't like him to show off his money. Like he's got this money because I really don't care if a guy has money because I have my mother. I could ask her for money.

The young people in this study do not tend to look for a sexual significant other to solve their problems.

SEX EDUCATION, CONTRACEPTION, AND AIDS

Sex education, contraception, AIDS, and teenage pregnancy are the controversial or problem areas that are associated with adolescent sexuality. Among the respondents of this study, however, no one spoke of being pregnant, being a parent, or even of knowing anyone in these situations—although they undoubtedly did. This was not the case in my study of less successful students. Respondents in that study included both young men and young women who had become parents. Forty percent of the teenage girls who drop out of school, cite pregnancy or parenthood as their reason (Pittman, 1988). The young women in this study obviously do not want to drop out of school. Jennie, in the "Boyfriends and Girlfriends" section, above, probably speaks for most respondents when she referred to pregnancy as something to be avoided.

The Status of Sex Education

The students in these dialogues, as were the less academically successful students in my previous study, seemed to be knowledgable about sex, sexuality, contraception, and AIDS. New York has successfully implemented sex education programs in the schools. There are training programs for teachers and instruction is mandated. While there is opposition to such programs in some parts of the country, such opposition is less apparent in urban areas. In fact, in spite of vehement objections by a small number of parents in New York, sex education seems to be expected in the schools by both parents and students. When asked who should have the responsibility of teaching young people about sex, Tony opted for schools.

> Tony: Well, parents don't have the knowledge of sex enough because it was different back then, right? And most of them are ashamed or too embarrassed to put it the right way for kids to understand.

As to how successful sex education is still remains to be seen. A successful implementation does not necessarily mean successful results. AIDS and other venereal diseases appear to be on the rise in the city, although not necessarily among high school students. I suggest that teenage pregnacy, at least in New York, is not primarily caused by lack of knowledge. But it seems to me folly not to teach human reproduction and sexuality in the schools. I suggest that no knowledge can be dangerous and I submit that few people seriously believe that knowledge of sexuality leads to a permissive attitude. The voices of these students seem to bear this out.

Views on Contraception

Whether it is taught in school or not, contraception and prophilaxis are facts of life. "Safe Sex" and condoms are topics addressed in popular media outlets such as MTV. The availability of condoms and related products—even on supermarket shelves—demonstrates that the market economy prevails. And not even those respondents who are not sexually active and who were opposed to premarital sex expressed any misgivings about this new phenomenon. In the age of AIDS, these young people appear to take a realistic and a sensible position. The voices of both young men and young women lead us to believe they have developed a sense of responsibility. Most respondents, when asked, seem to believe that both parties should take responsibility for birth control and prophilaxis but Kathy thinks otherwise.

> Kathy: I'm going to take it as my responsibility because I'm not going to let some guy get me pregnant or give me some disease because I feel it's his responsibility because he's a guy.

No one, however, addressed the issue of the availability of condoms in schools. This was a controversial issue in New York as well as in other parts of the country. At the time these data were collected (September 1990–May 1991), the program had, for the most part, not been implemented although it had been approved. Perhaps the availability of condoms, as discussed above, is not as controversial an issue to young people as it is to many adults.

AIDS as Conspiracy

Among students in a dropout prevention program in 1986–88, AIDS was often mentioned and discussed. Many expressed real fear of the disease. Even though AIDS is growing in minority communities faster than anywhere else in this country, the subject came up less among the respondents in this study. Those who were not sexually active were not overly concerned about it. However, a few young people spoke of a suspicion that is sometimes voiced in the African-American community.

> Interviewer: Certain black activists believe that AIDS was a disease created in a laboratory to minimize the black population. Many whites believe that the AIDS virus came from a monkey in Africa. Yet black activists believe that the AIDS symptom was always in the vaccine that they've been giving since 1960 something, in the Herpes vaccine because they gave gays the herpes B vaccination, and they give straight people a different vaccination. They believe there was something in those vaccinations, you know, that distinctly created . . . in a lab. What do you think about it? Do you think it's a disease created by man or that monkey in Africa or a freak accident? What do you think?
>
> Joe: I think that an unknown germ just came out and infected everyone.

Change Joe's "germ" to "virus" and his answer would be what we expect most people think. However, the same interviewer asked a number of her respondents the same question and four expressed the belief or, at least, the suspicion that AIDS was part of an anti-black conspiracy. These are achieving college-bound students. Moreover, some African-American students of mine at the City College have expressed similar views in class. The interviewer, a young woman, asked the same question in several different ways. Her interviewees seemed perfectly reasonable, truthful, and sincere.

> Interviewer: Some—like what you hear on [call letters of an African-American radio station]—some people believe that AIDS was a disease created by men to extinguish the black race. Some people believe it was a disease that just popped out of nowhere.
>
> Ginny: You know what I think?
>
> Interviewer: Yeah?
>
> Ginny: This may sound crazy, but I think the government created it.

In no way do I mean to diminish the impact of AIDS but perhaps the atmosphere that fostered these attitudes is even more destructive. A number of our successful young people, the people who will become the future leaders of the minority community, seem to believe that there are forces in this society, perhaps even the government, that are conspiring to exterminate African-Americans in the most horrible way possible. It is easy to dismiss such a conspiracy theory: there is no credible evidence for it; the disease is costing the society an enormous sum of money; a virus is nondiscriminating; only a lunatic would release such a disease on our population. But we cannot so easily dismiss the racial attitudes that produce, at least for some, totally different realities. We will discuss the realities of parents in this regard in chapter 5.

SEXUAL ORIENTATION

A frequent question that two of the interviewers asked was, what was the hardest problem you ever had to face. In a program where academic achievement is viewed as crucial to success, in a school where peers pressure good students to cut classes, in a city known for drugs and violence, Ken's hardest problem was being approached by a homosexual.

> Ken: All right I was going to propose—oh, I hate to use the term propose. However, I don't see it as any other way, but the way I see it, he kind of proposed to me. The faggot thought I was a faggot and he proposed to me. And it was kind of hard to get over that because I thought to myself why did it happen to me. Why me? Do I look like or walk and talk like a faggot?

Why was that Ken's *hardest* problem? Homosexuality is, of course, frightening to many adolescents. Sexuality of any type is new to them and, at a time when one is trying to forge an identity, what they consider deviance can be threatening. The sexual self is driven by powerful physical urges but has little experience in the world to draw from. Ken, above, was the same young man who said he would be reluctant to approach an attractive young woman because he was afraid she would "dis" him. The adolescent ego can be fragile and I think Ken is more typical than not. But is he typical in his attitudes toward homosexuality?

Every respondent who was asked spoke negatively about homosexuality. "Nasty." "Disgusting." "I don't believe in it." There were more graphic comments referring to specific acts of sodomy. Young women as well as young men shared these beliefs and no one spoke of knowing gays or lesbians. Yet New York has a large and politically active gay population. The African-American mayor attracted a great deal of media attention when he recently refused to march in an annual St. Patrick's Day Parade (a must for politicians in New York) because a gay contingent was excluded. More recently, the whole parade was jeopardized on this issue. Notable African-Americans like Langston Hughes, Bayard Rustin, and James Baldwin were gay. These young people, however, seem to have adopted the attitudes of society at large. It should also be noted that a number of these young people had strong religious affiliations and they may have been acting on those beliefs. We will look into this in chapter 8.

Among the respondents from my study of students in dropout prevention programs, no one voiced a sympathetic attitude toward homosexuality but a number of gay students were interviewed in that study and the subject could be discussed; although when it was, it was often tinged with humor. None of the young women in that study, however, mentioned it. African-Americans in that population seemed more tolerant than Latinos. I cannot say those students were actually accepting of homosexuality but they seemed to recognize its prevalence and they accepted the fact that there were gay people in the world.

In the earlier study, Latino students, mostly Puerto Rican and Dominican, were not very comfortable with the subject. A lesbian friend of mine who is Puerto Rican tells me of a common expression that her father—and many Latino fathers—used. Translated it means, (of my daughter) "better a whore than a lesbian." I could see no difference in attitudes toward sexual orientation between the African-American and Latino respondents in the current study. They were all opposed to homosexual acts as well as *being* a homosexual. This attitude may rightly be called "homophobic" but, it should be pointed out, no one expressed anger toward gays or lesbians; these do not seem to be the kind of young people who engage in gay bashing or who throw beer cans at the mayor because he supported gays (an actual incident that occurred at the St. Patrick's Day parade referred to above).

Because I am working with data from sixty-seven young people out of a school population of almost a million, I cannot say these attitudes are typical. Fine (1991) reports of a gay and lesbian alliance at a school she studied. I know of another city high school where one can outwardly be a lesbian. On the other hand, the Harvey Milk School in New York was established to protect students who were openly gay from being physically assaulted. At the City College, whose student body consists very much of students like these and which is the college that a number of the students in this study will attend, there was no gay or lesbian organization until 1991 and student attitudes seem very much like those expressed here. The Bisexual, Lesbian, and Gay Association at the City College has some fourty student and faculty members (of fourteen thousand) and there are obviously more gay and lesbian students but, except for an occasional anonymous letter in one of the college papers, many remain closeted.

THE SEXUAL SELF AND SCHOOL

The sexual self can become the dominant self in an adult or adolescent. A person, young or old, can spend all his energy seeking to fulfill his needs or acting on his drives. A young person's fantasies can overwhelm his consciousness while sitting in a classroom. For any young person, at least for some of the time, it takes considerable effort to concentrate on schoolwork and banish his or her intruding fantasies. Sexual behavior or even fantasies are likely to be the most exciting thing that happen to a young person.

All young people experience the emotional conflict between what society professes to believe about sex and their desires, which are often egged on and reinforced by their peers. As Kagan points out (1984), the conflict is likely to be cognitive as well as emotional. But the sexual self does not seem to be the dominant self in the lives of these young people. And neither are we able to say that it is dominant in the lives of their less academically successful peers. There is no indication that the young people in this study, for instance, repress their sexual drives and the others don't. They differ in that they do not feel the need to impress their friends about their sexual behavior. They do not feel the pressure to convince their friends that they have done something they have not.

In this sense, they have put sex and sexuality into a perspective that they can understand and can discuss with their peers. Another way of saying this is that they have developed a form of self-control; they are innerdirected. Some might argue that they have adopted the attitudes of adult society regarding sexuality and are, therefore, more outer directed. They are listening to their parents, their teachers, their ministers. We will discuss the idea of young people accepting the values of their elders further in chapter 10, but I think most observers would agree that these young people exercise some choice. Ken may not have a choice in deciding whether to approach a girl; his fears prevent him. But he is not acting (or failing to act) because of society's values and he will probably have more of a choice in the future. Gerald, who lost his virginity at seven, chooses now not to have premarital sex. The young women who complain about the "hungry guys" chose not to have sex, not so much, I think, because they are listening to society's voice but because of their determination not be manipulated by the young men.

They do not necessarily accept the societal premise that sexual activity is bad (Kagan, 1984). But in spite of their constant exposure to sexual situations presented in the most inviting terms in advertisements, in movies, and even on prime-time TV, in spite of the ready availability of condoms and other birth control devices, in spite of their knowledge of the sexual behavior of many of their peers, they are not overwhelmed by sex. It has a place in the lives of both those who are sexually active and those who are not. They are still developing their sexual selves but not at the expense of any other selves.

It may be, of course, that Erikson (1963) is right; the primary thrust of the adolescent is to find a career identity rather to engage in sexual behaviors. Most of these young people, as we saw in the last chapter, have made a tentative choice of a career and their career selves may be more dominant than their sexual selves. So too may their family and student selves. Because they have the sexual self in perspective, it is probable that they are able to integrate what in other young people may be competing and conflicting selves. It also seems that many get support from their friends in whatever sexual choices they might make. We will look into this in the next chapter, "The Peer Self."

3

The Peer Self

The importance of friends in the lives of adolescents is incalculable. Children can grow up without their parents; a number of the young people in this book have lived with only one parent all their lives. Without friends, however, both girls and boys would be desperately unhappy people. Vanessa speaks of two people, a best friend and a boyfriend, but she needs her best friend more.

> Interviewer: If your best friend wasn't around would you be able to go on or deal with the circumstances that you have to deal with now?
> Vanessa: I think I would need someone else to be talking to beside my boyfriend. I think if I had never met my best friend, it wouldn't be such an obstacle, but now that I have, I don't want to let her go.

Larry, too, voices this as he reflects on what his life would be like were he to lose his friends.

> Interviewer: Do your friends encourage you to do well?
> Larry: Always. But I think I'll never have friends like the friends I have now. You know, if I was to move or something, it would be like a major tragedy.

THERE ARE FRIENDS AND THERE ARE FRIENDS

What do these young people mean when they talk about "friends"? Do they mean a few intimate people? School people? Neighborhood people? A small circle? A large circle? They do not voice a typology and they do not even seem to have a consistent vocabulary to discriminate among peers. But they are well aware of the complexities of relationships and can make distinctions among their peers.

Good Friends and Bad Friends

Both these students and those classified as "at-risk" make a number of distinctions among those they call friends. Kara, below, has "good" friends, "best" friends, friends from junior high school, friends from high school. And then she has a special kind of relationship with the young woman who is interviewing her.

> Interviewer: Have your friends ever tried to press you into doing something either good or bad?
> Kara: Well. . .good, they've helped me—they don't pressure me. They tell me when I ask for advice, they tell me what's right or wrong. They tell me to do what I think is best.
> Interviewer: Those are good friends. I have a lot of friends in my high school, too, and I also have best friends and they basically tell me all wrong about guys, you know. I wouldn't put our friendship on the line; I would put our [Kara's and her] friendship on the line just to put you in the right direction, even if I would have to go as far as telling your mother and father. I would because I don't want you messing up. So you can relate to that in your own way.
> Kara: Yeah, I remember something my father told me. I got caught cutting class in junior high. He said he wasn't going to beat me or anything or even ground me. He was like, you're not destroying me or your teachers; you are destroying yourself. I'll never forget that.
> Interviewer: What about your friends? Do you think they would care if you dropped out of school?
> Kara: Well, my friends I had in junior high school, they didn't care what happened to me. I have to say the truth, even though they would be with me in a fight, you know, and say I care about you, but I don't think so. You see the friends I have in high school are different from the ones I had in junior high.

Students from an at-risk population voiced some of the same sentiments although none ever spoke of going to someone's parents to prevent a friend from "messing up." Like Kara, a young man in a dropout prevention program whom I have cited elsewhere (Farrell, 1990) distinguished between the friends he used to have and his current friends.

> The friends I have now is kind of like this. If we don't have no money, they know I don't have no money. They treat me in places and, you know, I treat them. You know, we all stick together. We back each other up. (p. 44)

But Kara is perhaps more sophisticated and astute. She is able to realize that even though friends might back you up in a fight, they might not *really* care about you, really care whether you drop out of school or not. Perhaps young women are better able to make this distinction. Being backed up in a fight might demonstrate more evidence of caring to a young man than to a young woman. In fact, as we will see below, the violent world of the urban high school may determine how and why one picks one's friends.

Violence is nothing new to urban high school students. It seems to ebb and flow through the years and between cities. In the 1950s and early 1960s, New York had many large street gangs staking claims to their "turf." Today,

Los Angeles has its Crips and Bloods while New York has somehow been spared of this. But, there is still violence and, if anything, the violence is more deadly. The incidence of firearms among the school-age population has made a qualitative change in violence so that it is unlike what has gone before. As I write this, a young man in a Brooklyn high school has just shot two others to death. Death can be anywhere.

One deals with violence by being ready for it or avoiding it. Kara's friends in junior high school were ready for it. Clint Eastwood is ready for it. People who purchase weapons—from firearms to mace—are trying to be ready for it. Carol Gilligan (1982), writing of Susan Pollak's and her study on violence in men's and women's fantasies as told in stories (Pollak and Gilligan, 1982), noted "the prevalence of violence in men's fantasies, denoting a world where danger is everywhere seen" (p. 43). But the respondents in this study, both males and females, by and large seek to avoid violence. Caring, to Kara, is keeping friends from dropping out of high school, not helping them in fights. To her interviewer, it is violating the peer code of not betraying confidences to adults and risking losing Kara's friendship if she thought it was in her friend's best interest. She seems to hold to higher values than even preserving a relationship.

Gilligan's (1982) analysis of men's story-fantasies indicates that her male respondents saw interpersonal relationships as easily replaced. Shawn, a popular young man in our study, seems to bear this out with his somewhat hard-boiled attitude on friends but also knows that he needs them. Impressed that Shawn is head of student government in his school, a collaborator comments:

> Interviewer: Wow, that means you've got a lot of friends.
> Shawn: They're not friends because I don't call them friends. They're companions, people that I study with because when we're studying, when we're in school—we don't go to school to, you know, talk about things that happened the day before in lunch—but we got a study group period.
> Interviewer: Are there any friends in school that influence you?
> Shawn: Well, I got a few friends who stayed by me when I went through a process that's really tough and I got friends that influence me to keep on and not give up, good friends. People are there when I'm down and when I'm depressed and sad but, you know, they're always there for me either to listen or there for me to cry. They're very careful, it's like they don't want to lose you in a way.

Loyalty, then, seems to be the most valued attribute in a friend but Germaine, a young woman, realizes that you pick the friends you are going to be loyal to.

> Germaine: Well, most of my friends are sweet. That's just about it.
> Interviewer: But you should have certain qualities when you're looking for friends because I know you don't pick anybody off the street. So what makes

your friend a friend? What is different from them from the people on the street?
Germaine: Well, this person—if I have a friend, I must be able to trust him
or her and, um, they must be loyal to me also.

Dangerous Acquaintances

Vanessa, whose comments on the importance of her best friend began this
chapter, also speaks of the downside of dealing with peers.

> Interviewer: Is there anything you would change about your school?
> Vanessa: Sometimes what really gets to me are the people in the school.
> Interviewer: Can you explain why?
> Vanessa: In Kennedy, there's many diffrent types of people. There's—I'm going
> to tell you straight out—hoodlums. Oh, let's do this, do that. Then there's
> academic people. There's different kinds of people and sometimes there's
> pressure; I admit some of these friends give me pressure. A lot of pressure
> comes from these people and it's a big school. If you had a small school,
> I think it would be easier for people. It would be such a small school that
> no one would think about doing this, doing that.
> Interviewer: Why do you think so many kids are messing up?
> Vanessa: Some of them because they don't believe in themselves, and some
> of them because they don't have ambition. Some of them because they let
> their problems really get to them.

Christian, a young woman, and Maria also speak of the possible influence
of peers on one's behavior.

> Christian: It's not only the environment. It's the people you associate yourself
> with. It's your peers. If your peers are cutting class then you will cut class.
> If your peers are going to class and succeeding in life, then you will succeed
> in life.

But Maria exhibits an attitude that is more resistant to peer pressure.

> Interviewer: Do you find people that will encourage you to play hookey?
> Maria: Yes, there's many, many people out there that will always ask me to
> play hookey and hang out and, you know, say it's just for one day. Tomorrow
> you can make everything up. But the truth is even if you do make it up, you
> still don't know what's going on. So it's better just to keep on going to school.

Unlike these two young women, Tommy, and possibly Larry, has
succumbed to the urgings of his friends.

> Tommy: If I know there's going to be something real good, I will cut. Like
> go to a party, a hookey party, I'll cut out of school. Or drinking I might cut
> out of school, but I don't drink. I might cut out of school, I'll say that. And
> if I just don't want to go to school, I don't go.

Larry does not say he has succumbed, but his description of peer pressure is more graphic than Maria's. One might think he is subject to more of it. It may also be that young men are more susceptible than young women.

> Interviewer: Have any of them or any other friends tried to pressure you?
> Larry: Like into drugs or something?
> Interviewer: Yeah, and like drinking.
> Larry: Oh man, some people—they get influenced—you know, they see the crowd, they see their friends smoking. I can't be out of the crowd, you know. They're going to think I'm queer or something. Some people smoke because they want to look cool.

Nerds

Those who are not cool are nerds. This term was used extensively by at-risk students. It is at best a term of humor but is often a pejorative. In a previous study (Farrell, 1990), students in a dropout prevention program frequently taunted those students they called nerds. The "nerds" in those situations were generally younger students who could do no more than retaliate verbally to the taunts. John, one of the respondents in this study, however, sometimes feels forced to do more.

> John: I'm in a special business program, you know, the kids in there have high grades and they're really into their classes.
> Interviewer: You don't have any particular problems in school?
> John: Well, I've had a couple of fights with kids trying to say I'm a nerd.
> Interviewer: You shouldn't let that bother you, take it as a compliment.
> John: I do take it as a compliment but when they try to get physical, you know, they call me a nerd and I don't mind, but when they try to push me around, I just can't take it and since I took boxing a couple of years back, and I just demonstrate to them. . . .
> Interviewer: Your skills.

It may seem difficult to believe that some young people have to defend themselves physically for being good students, and John may be an exception, but my student-collaborator who interviewed him did not doubt his story.

The term "nerd" seems to be applied more to young men than young women. Implied in it is a lack of masculinity. Nerds do what they are told by parents and teachers. It is usually a term of derision or mockery that even teachers and college professors use; many recognize it as a valid descriptive term and can joke about those so labeled. There have even been Hollywood films about such students where, as underdogs, they turn the tables on their oppressors. We must recognize that, although we as educators might not consider the respondents in these dialogues nerds, many of their peers do. The key question, then, is: does one have to be a nerd—especially, if male—to be successful in school? A refinement of that question would be: does one have to tolerate being called a nerd as a consequence of being a successful student?

In many inner-city schools, the answer to this question is yes. In many surburban or small-town schools, a successful student—especially if he has some athletic or social ability—can be a "jock." Penelope Eckert (1989) presents a fascinating analysis of jocks and burnouts in a Michigan high school which we will look at in chapter 8. She argues persuasively that the distinction is based on social class and is fostered by the administrative and social structures of schools. In inner-city schools, however, being a nerd has little to do with one's social class but being called a nerd might have a great deal to do with what class one aspires to.

The notion of social class is fuzzy to most of our respondents and is very much intertwined with race. As a high school teacher I found few students who could verbalize the difference between working and middle class although they were well aware that people were regarded differently. In the dialogue that began chapter 1, it was clear that both Sharon and her interviewer spoke of themselves as being "lower class." They realize they are have-nots but they seem not to believe that simply getting rich—by selling drugs, for instance—will transform their class identity. Students who aspire to be professionals have a definite picture of their future lives in the middle class. None of the at-risk students in my previous study had these aspirations and, I suggest, they had received many messages over their years in school in the form of criticism, poor grades, and tracking so that they have become convinced on some level, perhaps even an unconscious one, that class mobility will always elude them. It is natural, if not moral, that they might resent their more successful peers. How better can you insult those whom you resent than to imply they do not have the autonomy that you do because they are so adult-directed and, additionally, that they are somehow lacking in masculinity?

If sharing values with adults is being adult-directed, the students in this study *are* adult-directed; they do aspire to the middle class; they do succeed in school. One would not describe John, however, the young man who fights back physically, as lacking in masculinity, using the adolescent male connotation of the concept. In the last chapter, we saw that some number of our respondents were sexually active; others were not but were not by choice. Some had transcended the pejorative label of "nerd" and were not bothered by it. But they are a minority of students. Michele Fine (1991) writes of an urban high school where only 20 percent of those starting ninth grade eventually graduate. True dropout and graduation rates are not made readily available and are often impossible to determine but I suspect her figures are not atypical. With so few students experiencing success, it is probable that those who do will be labeled nerds.

Many of my students in teacher education programs at the City College of New York may have been considered nerds by their peers in high school, although few admit to it. But they are the people who will become teachers in a few years. Obviously, I do not think of them as nerds and both they and I realize they will have to become the models for the young people who follow them. Will they be able to attract students to their values and will their values be perceived as "nerdy"? I believe that my students, because they are mainly African-American and Latino, will be perceived as models by their students and will be able to dispel the notion that there is something wrong with those who succeed in school.

PEERS AND MORAL DEVELOPMENT

In my previous study on at-risk students I suggested that peer loyalty was the basis for moral development in their adolescence. Moral choices in adolescence are often forced because of a tension the young person feels between teacher or parent values and peer values. In analyzing this, I cited Lawrence Kohlberg's (1981) famous theory of the development of moral reasoning. Kohlberg hypothesized that people reason about moral decisions based on orientations that may be altered as they grow older. He presented these orientations as stages which may or may not be keyed to age. Each stage represents a higher order of reasoning, characterized as a "higher" order only because it takes in more variables and uses more and more of a social rather than an individual orientation in coming to a moral decision.

I outlined Kohlberg's six stages and suggested that both successful and at-risk students could be at the same level of moral development. They may be listening to different voices; for instance, some successful students might be concerned with their image to adults more than peers while at-risk students might be more concerned with the image they present to peers. I find, however, that the data from the respondents of this study are not easily analyzed in Kohlbergian terms; most seem to be in his third stage—conventional with a good boy–good girl orientation. We have seen that loyalty is valued by the interviewer of Kara, above, and by Germaine but there might be something above personal loyalty that is not easily explained by the influence of societal values or Kohlberg's postconventional reasoning.

Carol Gilligan, however, gives us another way of looking at the development of moral judgment which may be applicable here. I dislike thinking that there may be two separate systems of moral development, one for men and another for women which is often a popular interpretation of Gilligan's work. Gilligan (1977) writes of "two different constructions of the moral domain—one traditionally associated with masculinity..., the other with femininity...." (p. 60). But later she describes the "different voice" as "characterized not by gender but theme" (1982, p. 2). This theme is "care" which is described as the bridge between the selfishness of childhood and the responsibility of adulthood. Both men and women hear the different voices but women are often socialized to heed the "different voice" of caring for others.

According to Gilligan, with Kohlberg's theory, women in general and, as pointed out above, the young people in this book, the majority of whom are women, are often seen as making moral judgments on the third stage of his scale. This is the level of shared values and personal image. On the one hand, you do your homework because your teacher or parent will be disappointed in you if you don't. On the other, you may refuse to do it because homeboys don't do homework, only nerds do. This demeans the efforts of the successful woman as simply aiming to please someone else; or of the young man seeking somehow to make his own decisions as wanting only to look good to his friends.

Describing young people as making a transition from selfishness to responsibility, as Gilligan does, however, casts them in a different light. Although their teachers would probably describe most of the young people among our respondents as responsible, does that mean that unsuccessful students are irresponsible? I would hesitate to say so. Does describing the male students among our respondents as operating in a moral domain traditionally associated with femininity diminish them in any way? Obviously not. But I think it is fair to describe our respondents as responsible young people. They are responsible for their success. Perhaps they hear the voices of teachers and parents more than they do peers; perhaps Tommy, cited above, or the students in my previous study hear the voices of their peers more than those of adults.

We will see in the next chapter that many respondents in this study come from nurturing and égalité-based families that are, by and large, functioning well. This is in keeping with Fine's (1991) findings which she arrives at from analyzing the autobiographies of sixteen graduating seniors in an urban high school. While I had little direct evidence that the families of at-risk students in my previous study were malfunctioning, most of those respondents mentioned that they had conflicts with their parents. It might follow then that more successful students would tend to listen more to the voices of parents. In addition, their school success has probably won the approval of at least some of their teachers and one tends to listen more to the voices of those who approve of you.

Moral decisions of this group, in Kohlberg's terms, may be based on projecting a certain image to parents and teachers. But in Gilligan's terms, these students may be making a transition toward responsibility through caring. We will hear in the next chapter many voices speaking of a caring attitude toward their families. Does this mean then that these students "care" more than others? In my study of at-risk students, I wrote that the most positive and admirable behavior exhibited by my respondents was loyalty to friends. I have examples of very touching dialogue that demonstrates a real degree of caring for their friends. But friends are often transitory. If only 20 percent of the people you start high school with finish, many friends must keep disappearing from your life. As a result, the caring that respondents in this study seem to feel may be more directed toward family members.

The moral decisions of this population, therefore, might be based not so much on merely projecting an image to parents and teachers but by being responsible to their values because they are people worth caring about. The transition from selfishness to responsibility, writes Gilligan, to whom we will return in chapter 10, "requires a conception of self which includes the possibility for doing 'the right thing,' the ability to see in oneself the potential for social acceptance" (1977, p. 66). Peer loyalty, even though they value it, is *not* the basis for moral decision making in these adolescents. Germain, above, spoke of expecting trust and loyalty from a friend but also realized that she had to choose her friends and that most of her friends were ". . .sweet. That's just about it."

Peer Subculture

The great influence that peers have on adolescents have led some commentators to wonder whether there is a separate subculture of young people within the dominant culture. In my study of at-risk adolescents (Farrell, 1990), I pointed out that their values were often in opposition to the values of the encompassing culture, especially where school is concerned. I suggested that their language codes differed enough to often be undecipherable to adults in the dominant culture. Finally, using Bruner's (1986) hypothesis that there are two distinct modes of thinking, the narrative and the paradigmatic, I speculated that my respondents functioned mostly in the former mode while the process of schooling seeks to direct the development of the latter.

Different values, different language patterns, and different ways of thinking defined, I thought, a subculture that was distinct from the encompassing culture, especially if it could be determined that that subculture was in some way an adaptation to the exigencies of social and economic survival. And, indeed, the subculture gives young people a social life, access to sexual contacts, and a rudimentary, if not completely successful, job-seeking network. But the subculture can be maladaptive for some. Acting on peer values—not doing homework, cutting classes—when these values conflict with those of society, can result in dire educational consequences. If the adolescent is immersed in the peer culture and the peer self is her dominant self, she may reject societal values and engage in maladaptive behavior.

There was, however, no indication that the young people interviewed here are immersed in any kind of a peer subculture or that they even recognize a set of peer values that conflict with those of the encompassing society. They may be critical of societal institutions like school, as we will see in chapter 6, but they accept the positive value of education. We saw in chapter 1 that they see education as the way to career success and that the prospect of a career within the encompassing dominant culture drives their efforts in school. They seem not to have a conflicting set of values that is in any way maladaptive to their educations.

Their culture *is* the encompassing culture. This is remarkable in light of the racism that they know exists and the classism that they might suspect. We will see in chapter 6 that at least a few students believe they are being shortchanged by society in their education. Fine and Rosenberg (1983) found that dropouts were more critical of society than the successful students they call "graduates." Their "graduates," who they describe as "optimistic," can be equated to the students of this study. Their graduate "distinguishes 'us' from 'them,' and aspires proudly to the middle class..." (Fine, 1991, p. 135). The encompassing American culture is indeed middle class and our respondents believe they will have a place in it as well. And if all their peers don't, so be it.

SCHOOL SUCCESS AND THE PEER SELF

Although the peer self is formulated prior to the career self in a person's life, it has been overtaken rather quickly by the latter among most of the respondents of this study. We will see in chapter 6 that the student self is also a more powerful force in the lives of these young people. But the student self exists in some form as soon as a child starts school. In most young people a career self does not start much before junior high school and not usually until high school. At a time of budding sexuality when one is most concerned with how one looks in the eyes of others, it would seem that identity would center around the peer self. But somehow this has not generally emerged as the dominant self in the lives of our respondents, although it appeared to do so in the lives of at-risk students in my previous study.

Yet from the voices of these respondents, we can see that they are not socially isolated. They value their friends and many would suffer real loss without them. One wonders if they actually suppress the peer self in some way? Citing Gilligan, we saw that these young people are assuming more and more a sense of responsibility in their moral consciouness. Piaget (1965), himself drawing from Baldwin (1897), speaks to the appearance of moral consciousness as well.

> Moral consciousness appears when the self is no longer in a state of harmony, when there is opposition between the various tendencies that constitute it....Whence comes this lack of harmony? From the fact that sooner or later the child is compelled to obey the adult, and that in obeying he experiences something quite new....Obedience creates a new self, a fraction of the self that dominates the rest. (p. 388)

Although the phrasing of this passage makes those of us who call ourselves modern educators shudder—the very word obedience conjuring up images of coercion and punishment—it helps explain the suppression of the peer self. If we rephrase Piaget's last sentence into a more palatable idiom we might get something like, obedience (read: accepting the teachers' and parents' values) creates a career and a student self that is dominant among the other selves, especially over the peer self. If a student has no prospect of a career or if she has experienced very little school success she will not have developed much of a career or student self. The peer self then becomes a larger part of the self system and a young person's identity is more likely to revolve around her peers. I am Sonny's or Suzanne's or Spike's friend rather than I am a high school student or I am going to the City College.

Some commentators might interpret this analysis as a rejection of young people's autonomy. Fine (1991) states, "But we also need to worry about the racial, cultural, and class-based anesthetizing performed on those students who constitute the 'academic successes' of low-income urban schools" (p. 137). Are these students "anesthetized" when they obey adults or accept adult values and when they reject the values of many of their peers? I do not find my students at the City College, who, during their high school careers, were considered the " 'academic successes' of low-income urban schools" to be anesthetized. They are well aware of the force of racism and cultural imperialism in society. Is there a naivete, then, about the very optimistic students we encountered in chapter 1? Yes, but I believe they are aware of the injustices of society and the fact that they could be victims of those injustices. It may even be that knowledge of those injustices is one of the things that drives them. They are *choosing* to put effort into their educations. They could easily choose otherwise and find many peers to support them in their decisions. In this they are autonomous.

The peer self, then, may have been diminished in school settings as these young people developed. There is obviously a conflict in values between them and the other young people whose peer selves are their paramount selves. Since our respondents are a minority among their peers in holding their adult-oriented values, they carry a heavy burden. In addition to the burden of being so few and often objects of derision, they and their less successful peers must be aware—on some level—that they are accepting the values of the dominant white culture. Their teachers are, by and large, white; their peers are, by and large, people of color. At this time in their lives, however, they may not wish to confront that issue; their primary mission seems to be to succeed in school and lay the foundations of a career.

To do this, they may have to reject some of the values of their peers and some of their peers themselves. I believe Fine (1991) is correct in her statement that the "graduates" she writes about make a firm distinction of "us" from "them;" "us" being those who have achieved academic succes; "them" being the others. In the "Dangerous Acquaintances" section above, Vanessa spoke of hoodlums; Christian and Maria told how the wrong friends can do you harm. The young women among our respondents seem to be able to reject the "others" out of hand. Young men, like Tommy and Larry in the same section, do not do this so easily. Perhaps there is male bonding in cutting classes, going to parties, and experimenting with drugs and alcohol. Girls are generally thought of as being more "obedient," to use Piaget's term.

The young men who repress the peer self have a more difficult time than the young women. Shawn, whom we met above, we described as "hard boiled" about friends but was highly regarded socially. John felt he was pushed to the extreme of physically fighting. In such circumstances, it may be impossible to have both a strong peer self and a strong student self. With luck one might be able to surround oneself with a few like-minded friends. Larry and Vanessa, whose voices began this chapter, managed to do this and their friends became very important to them. But Larry did not think he would find new ones if he moved. Vanessa spoke only of two: her best friend and her boyfriend. Those who are less social and have less of a peer self may have to function as rugged individualists. Like Rafael, they may adopt a tough exterior which they voice when asked.

> Rafael: Friends don't hurt me in nothing whatsoever in school. I do good in school without my friends or with my friends.

Rafael may be a successful student but we wonder what price he has paid for that success.

4

The Family Self

Family relationships among the students in this book ran the gamut from debilitating conflict to supportive closeness but with many more people reporting the latter situation. Vanessa, who with some effort became a successful student, explains former difficulties with her mother.

> Vanessa: I always had different problems with my mother. We never really got along, always into arguments. And she would, at times, call me stupid, idiot, call me names and make me feel really bad about myself and, um, I had this stupid notion in my head that, well, if that's what she thinks then that's what I'm going to do and that's why I messed up.

Sherese, however, tells of a very different situation in a family that is larger than average and which has at least one characteristic of an extended family— multiple sources of support and comfort.

> Sherese: I live with my mother, my stepfather, two sisters and a brother. It's nice to have a lot of people in your house because you always have someone to talk to, and help you out with something, if you have a problem.

Sherese's family structure and size are not the norms among our respondents; she lives in a comparatively large family of six. The closeness of her family, however, is typical of many of those in our data. In my work with at-risk students (Farrell, 1990) I found that if the subject of "family" came up, virtually all respondents spoke of friction and of parents pressuring them to conform to certain standards. This was not the case among our respondents. On the contrary, the great majority of these students spoke positively of their family relationships. This was true no matter what the family structure was: nuclear, extended, or single-parent, although a number of those in the last category, as we shall see, seemed to have a more difficult time growing up.

FAMILIES AND CHILDREN

According to O'Hare, Pollard, Mann, and Kent (1991) of the Population Reference Bureau, a nonprofit and highly regarded educational institution, the average white household in the United States contains 2.6 persons; the average black household, 2.9; the average Latino household, 3.5. Of the ten million black households, however, only half were headed by a married couple. In 1980, 56 percent were but, in 1970, 68 percent. This percentage has also declined among white and Latino families in the last twenty years. These figures, it should be pointed out, were based on census data. A question that arises is, do the respondents in this study, successful students, tend to come more from those households that are headed by a married couple? This leads us to ask, as well, do less successful students tend to come from the other half? Since our respondents were not a random sample, our data cannot answer these questions. I have no tallies and they would be statistically meaningless with a nonrandom sample of sixty-seven students.

What we can address is how close the families are, how the members regard each other, how well they function. We can find out how the young people in our dialogues themselves describe their families. There is, of course, a range among the families of our respondents as to their attitudes and functioning. But even those whose home lives are less than perfect, we shall see, seem to care and think a great deal about their families. The dialogues they engage in and the questions they ask each other reflect this. One of my interviewers devised a question which she asked nearly all of her respondents. Following is one variation of the question with her friend Gloria's not uncommon answer.

> Interviewer: If there was something—this is a hard question. If there were something that you could tell someone before you died, who would you tell and what would you tell them?
> Gloria: Okay, you're going to be disappointed, but I think I'd tell my mother because, you know, she's the one who had me first. I gotta tell her I love her and...Julia and then my brothers.

Giselle's answer to the same question is similar and in her answer we get a realistic glimpse of a solid family that is not without its conflicts.

> Giselle: I would tell my parents...I hope that whatever I'd done had made them proud of me. I only lived to make them proud of me for whatever I did. These are the only two people, really, that I would speak to.
> Interviewer: Can you describe your parents?
> Giselle: They're years apart. They're like fourteen years apart from each other but they both think the same. They hardly ever argue with each other. They try to compromise. But they have views like when I want to go out—they hate the idea of me talking to guys.
> Interviewer: So is there a lot of yelling?

Giselle: No, it's quiet. I sit here and I hear about everyone's family life, how their parents beat up on each other, you know. And I thank God that my life is not like that at all. I can go home to a family that's willing to listen to what I've got to say or whatever. It's not like the Brady bunch but it's a good life.

From families, children acquire their basic ways of interacting with other people. This is more obvious with younger children than adolescents. One young woman, Carrie, changes roles with her interviewer when she asks how her family has told her to deal with conflict and gets a surprising response.

Carrie: Do you think that if someone had come up to you in your face and started to fight with you, do you think your parents would let you fight with that person?
Interviewer: Yeah, definitely. My father is the type of person that will say, don't hit first. My mother would say, step into their face, punch 'em and don't walk away. That's how my mother—they're completely opposite. My father is the type of person to say, if they hit you, kill. My mother says, don't wait for them to hit you. Kill them first. You see they're opposite, but I try to operate in between. I be myself. I don't be what my. . .I try to be myself. Because a lot of people think, oh, she's a pastor's daughter. She's so sweet. She can't do this. Well, don't try that with me.

If the interviewer does not fit the standard mold for a pastor's daughter, her family does not fit the mold either. It is unlikely that her parents advise her to "kill" but the family members are strong, assertive, and, I would guess, leaders in the community. They do not turn the other cheek nor should we expect them to. The interviewer is a successful and interested student who has chosen to actively take part in a project to find out about her peers. Her teachers, according to my teacher-informants who recruited the interviewers, do not consider her particularly aggressive.

Except perhaps for that of Vanessa, the first student quoted in this chapter, these families are functioning well. They serve as sources of inspiration for these young people. And time and time again, this inspiration is directed toward education. School is the way up. Most of the families in these dialogues value education and have passed these values on to their children. They seem to sense the demographic justification of this or know it from experience. In 1989, families headed by blacks, age twenty-five to forty-four, who are college graduates had a mean income of $54,400 which was 93 percent of the mean for white families in the same circumstances (O'Hare et al., 1991). College in New York city is accessable to virtually all through the City University at comparatively little cost, provided you get through high school.

Our respondents, apparently, also believe education is the major factor of later success but a number of them seem to want to achieve in school more to please their parents than anything else.

Jennifer: Well, I live with my grandmother, my mother, and my ten-year old sister. I have a little cat. I love my family life because my mother, she encourages me to finish school. She tells me what life is and what she's been through and everything. And you know, I wanna finish school too, to make her happy and, you know, to give her everything I can to satisfy her, her needs and everything.

Many of these students seem to be aided by encouragement, counseling, and other forms of support from their parents. They also seem to welcome it.

Interviewer: Does your mother encourage you to do well in school?
James: She regrets it when I do bad in school. Every time I get a low mark, she talks to me, makes me feel confident, and she tells me to try to do better and try your best because you're not different from anybody else.

Some parents take on a function of enforcement. They mean to see to it that their children do well in school. How successful they are as enforcers is debatable but many seem to have been able to pass on this value to their sons and daughters.

Houston: Everything in my house revolves around how we're doing in school.
Interviewer: Everything in your house? Everything in my house is enforced by education. If you're not interested in education my mother will do absolutely nothing. Nothing! You say hello to her. . . . No hello, please, go to school.

In fact, some students report that school achievement is central and often the only source of friction between them and their families.

Interviewer: How do you get along with your mother?
Paula: Nice.
Interviewer: So what does "nice" mean?
Paula: Nice is we get along together and the only time she ever bothers me about something is when. . . . She only bothers me about my grades and that's it.

All this is not to say that the families of nonachieving students don't value education. After researching students and families and after teaching school for many years, I have come to the commonsense belief that virtually all families want their children to achieve in school. But when a child has received poor grades for years, it might not make any sense to always try to be an "enforcer" to your adolescent; it might be counterproductive. Also, many poor and working-class families, as we will see in the next chapter, have all they can do to get through the exigencies of their daily lives. They, justifiably, often worry more about their children being involved with drugs and violence than about academic success.

FAMILY PROBLEMS

The family lives of even high achieving students have problems, disruptions, and frictions, from the not unusual adolescent distancing from adults to sibling troubles, to problems with the law or, conversly, with criminal elements. Family problems, of course, affect all the individuals in the family.

> Anna: I don't talk much with them. It's not that I don't want to, but I can't and I just can't think of things to say. I'm sure I love them and I appreciate what they've done. I just don't feel that I'm close enough to them. I know I could be closer, but I don't know what to do about it.

Anna's problem may solve itself. Adolescents' relationships with their families are often mercurial and what is a problem one day may not be one the next. An outside force, a change of fortune for good or ill, or a conflict may bring the family together. Jaime's problem, however, may be more difficult to deal with.

> Interviewer: Have you ever had any family problems that have gotten in the way of school? Can you give me an example?
> Jaime: For instance, bills, not enough money, things like that.
> Interviewer: Can you explain how this affects school?
> Jaime: When you have two parents arguing in front of you and your little sister, you have a lack of concentration on your school work and a lack....It interferes...

For some, it is precisely because they are family members that they have stresses and strains. One person's difficulty affects another.

> Cecilia: My brother, he's a nut. He's been getting in trouble lately: been having fights in school; not doing homework talking back to the teacher. We've done all we could to teach him respect. We've done all we could to teach him to act like a good kid, but I don't know, something backfired and now we're trying to just do it over. We have him reading because he doesn't like to read at all. I help him as much as I can on his homework. I'm trying to do the best I can, but I don't know, it just gets to me sometimes because he's my brother and I love him and I just don't want to see him go the wrong way. I don't want to see my brother in jail.

Jail is a reality for people in the inner city. The now famous statistic that there are more young black men in jail than in college shames us as a nation. The temptations—money, prestige, power—of illegal activity abound. Also, inner-city residents are more liable to be victims of crime. Bad things happen to good people. The so-called "victimless" crimes are also prevalent in this

environment. Two Latino students in one of our dialogues talk of the impact
of such activities on their parents.

> Interviewer: My dad tends to have half his paycheck wasted on a dumb machine
> or a play, you know. And my mom gets angry too, because there's a baby
> now. The baby's expensive.
> Louey: Today, mine's going to get a bonus from work. Should be at least about
> $6,000. You know, I hope he just pays off what he owes or whatever. Because
> the worst of anything is to see my father get hurt if he can't pay someone off.
> Interviewer: My father's always in jams. He gets out of one; he gets into one. . .

To most of us, this is the kind of thing we see in the movies or on television.
To some of our respondents, however, it is part of everyday life. How powerless
a young person must feel if he is afraid that his father is going to get beaten
up by gangsters. How little confidence he must have in the legal and law
enforcement system.

SINGLE-PARENT FAMILIES

The Bureau of the Census (O'Hare et al., 1991) reports that 54.8 percent of
black children in America live in single-parent households. twenty percent of
white children do as well as do 30 percent of Latino children. The large numbers
of single-parent families are attributed by many to be causal factors of social
problems even though such phenomena are more likely to be effects of yet other
problems. And, of course, living in a single-parent household affects children.
Anthony doesn't tell the interviewer precisely what has gone wrong with his
relationship with his parents but he obviously has been affected by disruptions
in his family.

> Interviewer: How is your relationship with your parents?
> Anthony: Well, honestly now, on the rocks.
> Interviewer: Who do you get along better with, your mother or your father?
> Anthony: Well, my parents are separated. I get along with my mother more,
> much more. She tries to understand me in ways that my father couldn't.

Cassie is aware of what she does not have. She does not think kindly of
the man who begat her but still misses not having a father.

> Interviewer: You're currently living with your mom in New York. Okay. How
> would you describe your relationship between you and your mom?
> Cassie: I think it's a good relationship because we talk to each other about
> what we have to talk about.
> Interviewer: Do you think it would have been better with your father or worse?
> Cassie: Worse.

Interviewer: Why do you say that?

Cassie: Because I don't like my father. We don't really get along. He's a butt-head.

Interviewer: Yeah, okay, um. If there's one thing you could change about your family life, what would it be?

Cassie: I'd change that I had a mother right here and a father with me, but my father's kind of a player. He has kids here, kids there. So it's like I would want a mother and father and whole sisters and brothers. I only have half sisters and half brothers.

Marianne is even more removed from her father. She does well in school, is a sensitive and realistic young woman, but she carries her loss with her. When asked by an interviewer if she had ever thought of suicide (not an infrequent question), Marianne was one of the few who responded in the affirmative and was willing to talk about it.

Interviewer: Would you say why?

Marianne: It was something with my mother. It's a long story. I never met my father, my real father. He used to be a drug addict and every time I did something wrong my mother would compare me to him. You're going to turn out to be just like him and things like that and one day I got upset and I told her I wish I was with my father and she got upset and everything like that. She was threatening me and telling me to get out of the house. She was kicking me out of the house and everything like that. I just felt the pain she was going through and I like took aspirin, almost a whole bottle. After I thought about it, I really didn't continue taking the pills. I just went downstairs to talk to my mother and explained to her why I told her I wished I was with my father.

Interviewer: Where is your father?

Marianne: I have no idea. I never met him. I've see pictures and things like that.

Interviewer: He's alive?

Marianne: I think so. I haven't heard anything that he's dead or anything like that.

Interviewer: Do you think that not knowing your real father has kind of put a strain on your family life?

Marianne: No, not really because I've lived so many years without him that it really hasn't disturbed me that much. I've thought about him, how he looks like, things like that.

But, of course, it has disturbed her and it has obviously put a strain on the relationship between her mother and her. Although it is a strain that may never go away, Marianne can still feel her mother's pain. She overcomes her own pain over the prospect of being thrown out of her house; she stops taking the aspirin; she goes back down to try to talk with her mother. Strained or no, these women are united. Their concerns are out in the open.

MOTHERS AND DAUGHTERS

Many of the young women among our respondents reported relationships with their mothers that were, at least from my male point of view, remarkable in their closeness. Whether this was a function of living in a single-parent situation or of adolescence, I cannot say. Perhaps in situations where people are thrust back onto themeselves, such closeness develops. For Katie, however, it was her mother who instigated this type of relationship.

> Katie: My mother, she surprised me recently. She started to actually talk to me like I'm a person and not her daughter. She jokes with me, which is something unusual. She tells me all her new dirty jokes. That's definitely new. She buys me, I'm surprised, clothes that she wants to wear, and these things look good. Because she can dress; my mother can dress.

Although her mother's behavior was something new, Katie had already admired her. Her statement, "she can dress," surely indicates someone she looked up to, at least from the point of view of physical appearance. She now seems gratified by the change and glad to have her mother as a friend.

We met Gloria above telling of whom she would want to communicate with were she dying. Her mother has become her confidant in a way that few mothers are.

> Gloria: Me and my mother is like sisters. Everybody says that we're like sisters. We wear each other's clothes. She and me talk about everything. There's not one thing about me that she doesn't know. And there's not one thing about her that I don't know.

Natalia also speaks of this kind of closeness but she is a little more reluctant than Gloria to divulge certain information to her mother.

> Natalia: My relationship with my mother? She's my best friend. I only really consider that I have two best friends in the world, other than my mother. My mother is really the best friend I have. I can talk to her about everything. Well, sometimes she tells me she's my friend but then, of course, she's a mother and so she's going to react like a mother at certain times. So, of course, I don't tell her *everything* everything. I'll tell her to the limit where I know she's not going to get mad at me, like when it comes to boys.
> Interviewer: I'm able to talk to my mom as a friend, too. And I always talk to her about boys. She thinks I'm guy crazy, but she knows who I like the most or whatever.
> Natalia: Well, things like that I can talk to her but when it comes to, like, I kissed a boy, you just can't tell those things to your mother, not yet. They're not ready to hear that.
> Interviewer: I think I'll tell my mom when I'm thirty.
> Natalia: I think I'll tell my mom when I'm married.

In light of the reality that single-parent households are increasing in the United States among all races, we may want to redefine the American family. We may want to think of the single-parent family as an alternative life-style rather than as a social problem. Surely the relationships that developed between some of these mothers and daughters were admirable. But for Marianne and Carrie who so sorely missed having fathers, I would rather ask if we could improve the socioeconomic and racial climate which must contribute to the absence of men in so many families. And I would agree with Jawanza Kunjufu (1985) who writes in his remarkable but neglected book, *Countering the Conspiracy to Destroy Black Boys*, that boys should be raised to become men who want to be involved in the nurturance of their children.

FAMILIES AS TRANSMITTERS OF CULTURE

Sociologists have long addressed (see Parsons, 1955) how compulsory education has displaced much of the family's role in the socialization process. However, one of the problems in urban education today is the school's declining ability to do this. Perhaps the family must take back its former role. The families of our respondents seemed to accept many of the values of the surrounding culture. By the surrounding culture again, I mean the North American, postindustrial, urban milieu in which they live either by choice or by circumstance. They believe in family, in education, in their children's ability to succeed. They see the city as a perilous place. Judging from several respondents' negative attitudes toward the Gulf War, they do not seem particularly patriotic or political. But we will see that many of them have strong religious affiliations.

How do the parents in these families pass on their values to their children? Are some families better at this than others? I have suggested elsewhere that parents of at-risk children at least verbalize their belief that education leads to future success. In fact, I think many of the family conflicts referred to by at-risk students emanate from children's reluctance to accept parental-societal values. It would seem that the parents in this study have passed on to their children positive conceptions of education. Our respondents seemed to accept the values of their families referred to above: family, education, and their own ability to succeed.

Values are passed down by parents, I would think, by telling, by modeling, by negotiation, and by conflict. Diana Baumrind (1973) developed what has become a well-known typology to characterize families according to the ways they deal with their children. Baumrind says families are authoritarian, authoritative, or permissive. Authoritarian families stress obedience to their children and seem to be driven by the desire to preserve order. Authoritative families are rational and deal with their children in an issue-oriented manner. They affirm and accept the child but set standards for future conduct. Permissive families are affirmative, accepting, benign, and they give as much freedom to the child as possible that is only limited by strictures that provide for for the child's physical survival.

Baumrind cautions that many families do not easily fit into her classifications. She has seen, for instance, noncontrolling, passively accepting families who are cool and uninvolved; these were not her idea of a permissive family. I am not able to use Baumrind's classifications on the families of our respondents from the data. But I believe families can be generally thought of as passing down values in one of two modes: authority-based or egality-based. And within these modes they can be nurturing or harsh. This would make for four categories. It should be realized, of course, that these are tendencies rather than hard and fast categories. Parents in both kinds of families use all four of the means listed above to pass on values. They can tell or dictate to the children what is right and wrong; they can model their values unconsciously or by being conscious examples themselves; they can negotiate with their children in a manipulative or nonmanipulative fashion; they can engage in conflicts with their children which may or may not be resolved.

I believe we can use this four-category system on the families of the eighteen respondents quoted in this chapter to determine something about the tendencies in their families. While there is not enough data to classify the families of Anna, Jaime, and Louey, we can make some tentative conclusions about the others. Vanessa describes a harsh mother although it is not clear if the family is authority- or egality-based. Carrie's interviewer, the pastor's daughter, speaks of an aggressive family which can be both harsh and nurturing but is probably authority-based. Houston speaks of a harsh and authoritative mother, at least about education. But fully twelve of the respondents speak of nurturing, egality-based families. Although we cannot say that this is the norm for successful students, it would seem to be helpful to a student to have such a family.

Robert Beck and Denis Wood have produced a remarkable body of work on family socialization based on microethnographic data (Beck and Wood, 1993; Wood and Beck, 1993) that is now coming into print. They believe that values and, in fact, culture are passed down by families in conflict situations. Drawing from Toulmin (1963), they see family conflicts as being resolved in situations that they metaphorically call "courts of reason and inquiry." Key to the passing on of values is the realization of the intent of the participants in the court by each of the other participants. This recalls George Herbert Mead's (1934) writings on the relationship between self and society and the learning of how to take the perspectives of others.

Beck and Wood, in one case, analyze a conflict in a middle-class nuclear family with two preadolescent sons. In a detailed microanalysis of a conflict situation they are able to justify that the parents took on very specific roles in a spontaneous situation: the mother as cultural authority and social historian, the father as a language and logic pedagogue. The family was classified as authoritative according to Baumrind's typology but nurturing rather than harsh even though, at one point, the mother slaps her son. How successful the whole socialization process was cannot be determined. The goal was to eliminate physically aggressive behavior of the older toward the younger son. If the boy gained an intellectual understanding of his behavior, he also had a model of physical aggression directed against him by his mother.

The families of our respondents are not all able to set up "courts of reason and inquiry." In an intense relationship as with Marianne and her mother, there are no arbiters, no historians, no pedagogues. The two women are isolated in a dyad and dyads promote passion, a passion of conflict and a passion of love. While our data did not contain actual family interactions, only the retelling of them, we can only make some inferences on how these families passed on values. It would seem that the families of our respondents passed down values in an egality-based rather than an authority-based mode and that they are nurturing rather than harsh. In my previous research with at-risk students, I did not find any mention of harsh treatment of children either. Giselle, above, speaks of families she has heard about in which the members "beat up on each other." Even assuming that such situations will tend not to be reported in dialogues, I believe that our respondents, overall, are treated benignly by their parents.

From the dialogue excerpts of this chapter, then, it would appear that the families of our respondents tend to be nurturing and egality-based in the classification system I have proposed. Like in other families, the parents of our respondents *tell* their children of their values. James's mother makes him feel confident. Jennifer's mother tells her what life is. The pastor's daughter makes inferences from what her parents say about dealing with conflict. Houston's interviewer reports that his mother goes beyond telling him to succeed in school; she is more authority-based than the other families and "enforces" her values by witholding favors.

Giselle's parents set an example of how to get along. Katie emulates her mother if only in dress. By modeling they pass on their positive beliefs in the family and the ability to succeed. But, of course, bad examples can be modeled. Louey and his interviewer tell of their fathers gambling away money and otherwise acting irresponsibly. Negative examples can have positive results in causing children to avoid the unwanted behaviors. Carrie and Marianne have fathers who did not stay with their wives. Their distress makes us wonder whether they will be able to avoid this and effect stable family relationships with their future men.

Even though Natalia calls her mother her "best friend" there is negotiation involved in their relationship. They're open and discuss things but there may be a tacit agreement that they don't share everything. Other respondents spoke of being rewarded for good schoolwork. The unstated negotiation is, if you do well in school, I'll do such and such for you. The young man who interviewed Houston speaks of negotiation even with his authority-based parent. She will do things for him if he does well in school.

Marianne tells the most graphic story of conflict. She needed to stop her mother from comparing her with the father she had never met but yearns for. Her mother threatens her with the ultimate betrayal—the end of nurturing. She, in turn, threatens her mother with a similar kind of betrayal—living with her father. The conflict is resolved by Marianne herself taking the perspective of her mother, perhaps because she may well be a mother someday, and tries to help her mother take *her* perspective.

Our respondents seem to have their share of poor or no role models, conflicts, and even some authoritarian influences. We cannot say whether at-risk students have more or less of these than our respondents. We cannot say that parents of at-risk students are less involved or noncontrolling with their children than the parents in our data pool. Both sets of parents verbally espouse the same values. The interaction of the peer self and the family self may be different for both groups. Somehow our respondents have accepted parental and societal values; they realize the intentions of other family members and they are able to take their perspectives. They live in functioning families and they contribute to making them function.

FAMILY, PEER, SEXUAL, AND CAREER SELVES

With less academically succesful adolescents—and even with successful ones—the family self is often in conflict with the peer and sexual selves. The peer self may say, cut class; the family self may say no. The peer self may say, try drugs; the family self struggles against it. But the family self here is formed by nurturing parents who are generally supportive of their children and their children's education. The peer self that we encountered in chapter 3 was also supportive of education and opposed to such activities as substance use. Also, the friends of our respondents seem to come from families with similar attitudes as theirs. The family and the peer self can be successfully integrated.

Integrating the family self with the sexual self is a little more difficult. If we are to believe Gloria's statement that there is "not one thing" that her mother doesn't know about her, she may have successsfully integrated these selves. Even those with close relationships are probably more like Natalia who didn't tell her mother "*everything* everything." Giselle wants her parents, who are willing to listen to what she has to say, to be proud of her. She admires their marriage, calls her family situation "a good life," but seems to accept the fact that they hate the idea of her "talking to guys."

And we have seen in chapter 2 that our respondents appeared to be quite mature about their sexuality. Either they were sexually active or they weren't and those who were at least voiced the belief that prophilaxis and contraception were the responsibility of both partners. If their sexual and family selves were not completely integrated they were generally not in conflict. Perhaps, like Natalia and the young woman who interviewed her, they foresaw an integration of these selves later in life, "when I'm thirty," "when I'm married." Perhaps that's the way of most women and their mothers. Worldwide, women are often not regarded as equal to their mother by their cultures until they become mothers themselves.

The family self does not often seem to be in conflict with the career self. We have seen that many of our respondents voice an interest in a career in the professions. Families do not usually quarrel with their offspring in those kinds of choices. None talked of living in Paris as an artist; none were drawn to the performing arts (New York has an excellent high school for that kind of talent); none were revolutionaries; none were involved with drugs or criminal activity. More importantly, as we have seen in chapter 1, because they were able to envision careers for themselves and presumably verbalize them to their parents, their parents could see that they had a direction. It was this direction that appeared to be lacking in my investigation of at-risk students.

Anna may have felt distanced from her family; Anthony's relationship with his was "on the rocks;" Louey was afraid for his father; Marianne took almost a whole bottle of aspirin over the conflict with her mother. But they loved, cared, and thought about their families. And most communicated with them. Elsewhere I have suggested that complaining about parents may not be uncommon in adolescent-to-adolescent dialogues and that academically at-risk adolescents were no different from any other adolescent population. I said that the necessary desire to be independent often conflicts with parental strictures. What underlay these suggestions, I realize, was the old Sturm und Drang theory of adolescence; adolescence is, of necessity, a period of upheaval.

But these adolescents do not, by and large, complain about their parents. Perhaps they see their independence in their future success. Perhaps they are better at dealing with delayed gratification than their less successful peers. But they do not often mention parental strictures, let alone conflict. There is little evidence of adolescent rebellion. Are these adolescents different from other adolescent populations or are their families different? As Tolstoy said, "All happy families are happy in the same way. Unhappy families are unhappy in their own special way."

5

Interlude—The Voices of Parents

The voices of the young people in our dialogues gave us a picture of their family lives but not, of course, a whole picture. In spite of the fact that, as we have seen, they generally spoke well of their families, we wonder what their parents think. According to these voices, their parents supported them in matters of career choice and, I suggested, probably transmitted to them or at least reinforced in them their beliefs that school and career were interlinked. Were we able to listen to parent-child dialogues, as did Beck and Wood (1993), cited in chapter 4, we might be able to find out just how these beliefs were handed down and reinforced. Obviously, such dialogues occur in the home or in other family situations and would be difficult to obtain, at least in the numbers of respondents in this book, but we do have data that consist of sixty parent-parent dialogues. These dialogues address their attitudes toward school and the exigencies of their lives as they cope with the formidable task of raising children in the inner city.

During the 1990–91 academic year, three teachers, two of whom were parents themselves, one parent who was not a teacher, and I conducted a study using the same research methodology that is the basis for this book. The teachers were my graduate students and they and the other parent were my paid research assistants. Parents tape-recorded dialogues among themselves and other parents in schools their children attended, in schools they taught in, and in other schools as well. My colleagues interviewed sixty parents who had children in twelve elementary, eight junior high, and six senior high schools in Manhattan and the Bronx. Probably none of these interviewees were the parents of the young people who were the respondents in this book. All, however, were African-American or Latino; half were single parents, including five men. A few of the interviews were conducted in Spanish and translated by one of my colleagues, Angela Hernandez, who is both a teacher and a parent. All dialogues were professionally transcribed and the three teachers and I analyzed the data following the procedures outlined in the Introduction and the Appendix of this book.

The voices of parents differed considerably from those of the young people in the previous chapters. Those respondents were interviewed by friends and, perhaps as a result, were much more forthcoming about personal problems and the intimate details of their lives. Perhaps because of the life-stage they are in, they are more self-reflective. Adolescents, according to Erik Erikson, are searching for an identity. The parents, however, spoke more of others than themselves. Few of them mentioned, and then only briefly, interpersonal problems with their children, whereas some of the young people detailed such problems. There seemed to be three types of parent voices in the dialogues: fearful and harried voices, critical voices, and hopeful voices. Within each type of voice there was a variety of concerns. And some of the same people spoke with more than one voice.

FEARFUL AND HARRIED VOICES

Fear was the dominant emotion expressed by parents and this was not limited to those with children of any specific age. Some feared for their children becoming involved with drugs, others feared them becoming involved with the wrong people, but most feared violence. They also referred to the difficulties of their daily lives. It is difficult enough to be a parent, let alone a parent in the inner city.

Violence

The major concern of virtually every parent interviewed was the safety of their children. While the perception of violence in inner-city schools is probably out of proportion to the actual number of incidents, violent incidents, including murder, have occurred. It is so unthinkable that a young person could actually be murdered in a school building that many parents, I suggest, simply cannot cope with it. Such a crime always gets reported on the evening news and the tabloids headline it often in the most shocking terms. Mrs. Patterson is an African-American woman on public assistance with eight children, seventeen, fourteen, twelve, ten, nine, seven, six, and four years of age. Although there were two large families in our data, a family that size is not typical among our respondents. Mrs. Patterson is apparently somewhat hardened to violence; she describes a terrifying incident but only sandwiched within the context of two of her children's discipline and academic problems in school.

> Interviewer: How about your son in junior high?
> Mrs. Patterson: He gets into a fight and he gets suspended; the other kid don't.
> Interviewer: Do you feel they have adequate discipline there?
> Mrs. Patterson: No and it's not safe. Yesterday, this person got shot.
> Interviewer: (Surprised) So that was the incident that was in the paper. A fifteen-year old boy got shot over a girl?
> Mrs. Patterson: In the chest. And my son told me. "Mommy, I just left him. I just left him and when I came back he was shot."

Interviewer: So you fear for the safety of your children?

Mrs. Patterson: I fear for the safety of my child. My daughter goes to Morris High. It's not safe. They want to put her in the GED program. I want her to go to school.

Fear of violence seems to be a preoccupation for a number of parents. I cite only three but virtually all parents spoke of it. Mrs. Lopez is a housewife, has one daughter, and says she will not have any more children "because of the way the world's going."

Interviewer: You don't work, right?

Mrs. Lopez: I don't lay at home and relax all day. Then I wouldn't feel safe. If my daughter's in school all day and I can't be safe in my house thinking she's going to be here and there's like no security.

Interviewer: Are you fearful of the neighborhood?

Mrs. Lopez: Too many kidnappings, too many killings. I've lived all my life here. There's drugs everywhere. There's loonies everywhere. I don't want anything to happen here the same way it happened down in . . . .down the hill with that little girl [referring to the alleged murder of a child by a homeless man that was headlined in the daily newspapers and on the evening news].

Another Hispanic woman speaks of the fear she feels for both her children and husband.

Mrs. Rodriquez: And living in fear. I'm living in fear because where I live is not that great. There's too many crimes going around here, muggings, killings, and I've seen a lot of friends go. And I'm afraid, I'm afraid. My husband also went, well, the father of my kids. You know, he works towing cars and I'm afraid of that too and I fear that he ain't gonna show up some night. And my kids are afraid. They don't want to go out on Halloween. They fear and I fear for them. You know, I fear that they fear and I hate the fact that they fear like that.

A woman from the Dominican Republic tells of hearing gunshots on the street and hiding behind cars. She is not alone when she speaks of kidnappings and believes there should be more police and more security guards around the schools. It is a characteristic of schools where there is a large first-generation Dominican population to see crowds of parents outside elementary schools at dismissal time. They call out to their children, often try to touch them when they are in line, and escort them home. Many recent Dominican immigrants come from rural areas in their country where violence is not common. What they hear and experience in New York is often a deep culture shock for them.

The fear of violence impacts on education in other ways. In the next section and again in chapter 7, we will see both parents and teachers critical of other

parents who never come to school, never come to meetings, never come to
parent-teachers nights. One parent explains one of the reasons for this to an
interviewer.

> Mrs. Gifford: The parents don't show up at the school board meetings.
> Interviewer: The Community School Board?
> Mrs. Gifford: Even the PTA doesn't go. In the evening, everyone's afraid to
> go out in the evenings.

Even if the perception exceeds the reality, violence is all too real in the inner city.

The Exigencies of Daily Living

Violence and the fear of violence, then, can interfere with children's education.
But so can day-to-day survival, paying bills, interpersonal problems, and the
daily inconveniences of living in a city. Half of the respondents were heads
of single-parent families. This, as we have seen in the last chapter, is the national
average for African-American families. And while a single-parent family can
certainly be a happy, healthy, and well-functioning unit, few would deny that
it is generally a more difficult living arrangement than a happy and healthy
two-parent family and this difficulty obviously impacts on the children's
education. A Dominican parent speaks to this and what she sees as its effects
on her daughter's schooling. Being a single parent, she had to send her daughter
away in a time of crisis.

> Mrs. Ortiz: In my case I really don't know what's wrong with my daughter.
> I think perhaps that it's because she was separated from me when she was
> about a year and three months old because I sent her from here to Santa
> Domingo with my father for three months because I was about to lose my
> second pregnancy and she always wanted to be carried by me and then I started
> spotting and I had to stay in bed for a month.
> Interviewer: Yeah, my daughter craves affection. Her father doesn't give her
> any but she's more attached to him than me.
> Mrs. Ortiz: That is normal. My kids used to blame me for the fact that their
> father wasn't living with me.

Having less money also impacts on families and children's education. With
but few exeptions, the respondents in this study have incomes below the national
average and many below the poverty line. Rents in New York are high yet few
complained of not having enough money. My colleagues, however, who
interviewed them, assured me that finances were a major concern. They believe
more money should be spent by government on education but they do not seem
to be asking for anything more for themselves. Doubtless, even though most
do not refer to it, some percentage of the single parents among the respondents
were on public assistance and I can attest from having been a social worker
that living on what makes up a family allowance is extremely difficult. Even

those who work must find this difficult. And putting food on the table must have a higher priority than education.

CRITICAL VOICES

There were many critical remarks among the voices of parents. There was criticism of the schools and the school system. But there was more criticism of other parents and the social system. The most devastating criticism, however, was that there is a deep and continuing racism that impedes the best efforts of minority group members.

The School System, the Teachers, the Curriculum

Criticism of the school system came from many parental sources. When an interviewer asked a custodial engineer with a twelve-year-old boy in her school if he thought the school system will fail, he shot back, "Not *will*, it has been failing. Look at the conditions of the school building. They look like dungeons!" A security officer with three successful children, seventeen, sixteen, seven, in the system said that classrooms were too crowded and there was no unity among staff members. Teachers, she said, did not talk much to her. "In a school, everyone should be a family."

An African-American woman who raised her three elder children, seventeen, twelve, seven, as a single parent but who was recently married, is critical of the curriculum and of the lack of programs.

> Mrs. Smith: They need more activities, more curriculum to their African background and such as that; they don't teach them totally correct; they need to make classrooms much smaller. One teacher can't really sit down and teach thirty-three children, it just can't be done. My boys, [one graduating] I have trouble with both the boys...they really are...they just need more attention in the school system and someone to talk to.

Mrs. Patterson, whom we met above, seems to have mixed feelings about school and teachers.

> Interviewer: How do you feel about the New York City school system?
> Mrs. Patterson: It's not really good because some teachers will teach the children right and some won't. And you know when it's time for them to take the test the children can't take them because they haven't been learning and they need to cut some of these holidays like Jewish holidays; you know two or three days out of school is unnecessary. They need a lot of changes here.
> Interviewer: OK, like what for instance?
> Mrs. Patterson: I'm one of the parents that likes to sign homework every time I see it and I tell them to call me if there's a problem but the teacher should deal with it in the classroom. Instead of always calling the parents, the teacher should know how to handle children.

A male, Puerto Rican, single-parent, salesman and clothing designer speaks of the predicament of his only daughter who is in the seventh grade.

> Mr. Hernandez: If you live in a low-class, high-minority neighborhood, you find the schools are less well equipped for the children. The junior high school in Harlem which my daughter attends, it's an overcrowded school. The teacher has thirty-five students and it's all done in one classroom.
> Interviewer: You mean there's no departmental program?
> Mr. Hernandez: No, because of the overcrowding problem, the different teachers come to her room. I feel at the present date that she's suffocating inside that one room. Education should be where there's an open atmosphere, not where a person is caged or in jail. Education should be a thing of want and free vibes.

Mr. Hernandez went on to tell of being bounced around among three schools when he first tried to register his daughter in the system.

> Mr. Hernandez: One school was very nice. It was a nice setting, across the street from a park—looked ideal but she wasn't in that district. The second school I went to you could smell the urine on the walls outside, you could see bums and low-class people hanging around the school. I said to myself, no way will I allow my daughter to go to school there.

Obviously, the criteria of choosing a school are somewhat different for parents in the inner city than those in more affluent environments, especially if one knows little about how the system operates and what parent options are. In the final chapter of this book I will describe the kind of school—one with the "open atmosphere"—that Mr. Hernandez seemed to be yearning for.

Finally, two parents complain of school. One, who is a teacher herself, speaks of not getting cooperation from her daughter's school.

> Mrs. Ortiz: I asked them to lend my daughter the books and the way the assistant principal went, "The books!" The way he stressed that and the tone of his voice he used, I didn't like. So he says, which books. Well, I say the books she's using in class. And he told me they could not lend the books because if a child takes the books home, the child will know the stories and will be bored in class and will not get anything from the lesson.

An African-American single parent was shocked by the remarks of a principal. "One principal had the gall to say in a meeting that he didn't mind being the lowest reading score because that way he gets more money for remedial help."

Parents and Society

But most parents were more critical of other parents and of society than they were of schools and teachers. A married father with two children blames other parents.

Mr. Williams: What I really think is the children are not getting good grades is because of their parents; the parents are not meeting with the teachers. They are not keeping up with what their children are doing in school and that has a lot to do with their children's learning; they have to have help at both ends.
Interviewer: Have your kids' teachers been doing a good job?
Mr. Williams: They have good teachers due to the fact that I was always available. I have found out that when a teacher knows there is a parent at home that cares about their children, they will give them extra support.
Interviewer: What about the principal or assistant principal?
Mr. Williams: They're all very good. They're supportive.

Another parent, a working African-American women with five children echoes this.

Mrs. Gifford: I'm a strong person and I don't believe in giving something for nothing and the problem we have in schools—and you know I don't want to demean anybody—is that these parents they don't work and they get a check from the welfare. They don't have to get up early in the morning or whatever and they feel guilty. And whatever thing the kids want they give it to them without the kids working for anything. And I don't think that should be so.

Many people look back to better days. A father of three, two in high school, himself a high school graduate and employed as a cook, is one of these.

Mr. Ruiz: There was more respect and value for a teacher who was an educator than there is value now. It seems that today in the nineties, teachers find themselves having more problems with students because of the problems dealing with communities.
Interviewer: So you think this is a societal problem?
Mr. Ruiz: Yeah, dealing with the community and being a parent myself, a lot of kids today are being brought up into a third generation on welfare. And all the negative elements in society: the drugs, the crimes. Why should a child go to school to learn—to say, become a fireman when you can make fast money on the street, dealing in drugs?
Interviewer: How can the government help the school system? How can we give children some kind of hope?
Mr. Ruiz: One time junior high schools had like career guidance where a kid will be invited to some kind of industrial company, to see how it operates, how people work for a living, to see what would be their goals. Maybe I could hold a piece of the pie, own my own house, have a nice car, have a base for when I get old.
Interviewer: Yeah, because I'm a teacher. If they live, let's say, in the ghetto of Harlem, South Bronx or whatever, they see the burnt-out buildings everyday, the drug dealers, the homeless, the corruption.

We will see in chapter 7 that many teachers also blame parents and society for problems they encounter in the schools. In the last section, parents spoke negatively of some teachers but directed most of their criticism toward the school system. Personal complaints were addressed to administrators rather than teachers. By and large, there was little personal antagonism directed toward specific teachers. One of the major reasons why this parent study was undertaken was that a previously completed study of teachers by teachers (see chapter 7) indicated that teachers had a great many negative feelings toward parents. This is unfortunate and should be remedied but, fortunately, most parents do not voice reciprocal negative feelings toward teachers.

Racism

Ten of the respondents and three of the interviewers in this study spoke of racism in the schools, in the system, and in American society in general. They believe that racism is to blame for the problems of education. Mrs. Patterson, the woman with eight children whom we met above, referred to this more than once and in a number of different contexts. It was she who was upset about too many Jewish holidays.

> Interviewer: What about the principal?
> Mrs. Patterson: He's not a good principal. I know these black children did something good somewhere and when the awards are given out, they're always given to Puerto Ricans.
> Interviewer: So you feel the school is prejudiced?
> Mrs. Patterson: Very prejudiced. It has always been. My sister was going there and it was like that. You know I'm not supposed to be in school unless there's a cop with me? Why? Because me and the principal had an argument. He pushed me when I was pregnant. I pushed him back, you know? All because he said my son disrespect him and I was trying to rectify my son in front of him. Teachers don't respect kids and they have no discipline.

Mrs. Gifford, the working mother of five, seems well-informed on the distribution of city resources. She takes racism above the personal level.

> Mrs. Gifford: I tell you that District 10—the district where they have white people—they get more money than us. They have less children.

District 10 in New York City, which will be referred to in the next chapter, was identified by Jonathon Kozol (1991) in his damning book, *Savage Inequalities: Children in America's Schools*, as a district in which schools with a predominantly white population are given more equipment and have markedly better facilities than those with a predominantly minority population. Mrs. Gifford became aware of that without reading Kozol.

A Baptist minister in a prestigious Harlem church, who is also a parent, was interviewed. He is a highly educated and outspoken community leader and he offers some startling remarks when he speaks of racism as deliberate, pervasive, rampant, and destructive.

Reverend: Even though 70 percent of the children in the school system are black or Hispanic, less than 10 percent of the educators or principals are. In other words, about 80–90 percent of school administrators who are supervising the education in 70 percent black and Hispanic communities are white.

Interviewer: Do you think students are discriminated against?

Reverend: The school is a reflection of society. I think the problem of the school system is tied to this conspiracy to destroy black children in this country. . . . It all ties up in a subtle national agenda to make sure that these blacks or Hispanics, you don't educate them too much. Keep them down so that in the future they will not be able to compete economically with their children.

Interviewer: Is the Board of Education part of this?

Reverend: There's no moral system attached to the Board of Education in this city.

In chapter 2, we saw high school students who seriously considered whether AIDS was created in a laboratory and deliberately spread by the government as a means of destroying black people. To white people, this seems preposterous but adolescents inquire about a great many things. If one has a lack of knowledge and experience, a notion like AIDS being spread by the government is no more strange than some of the plots in movies or on TV. But here, adults speak to personal and systemic racism and a highly respected community leader speaks of an actual conspiracy he belives to exist to destroy black children. The notion of such a conspiracy appeared in Kunjufu's (1985) book, mentioned in the last chapter. The reverend is certainly not alone in his belief.

No one would deny there is racism in American society. And we will see in the next chapter that school systems discriminate against minorities. Few whites and few policymakers of any race, however, would accept a conspiracy theory. But obviously there is a perception among some, if not many, minority members that they are consciously and systemetically discriminated against. The parents here are involved with their children's education and the young people in the previous chapters were successful in it but they apparently have a great lack of trust in the schools, in school systems, in local and in national government. I will not speak to conspiracy theories here except to point out that many suggest the plight of minority children could not be much worse even if there were a conscious conspiracy. Something must be terribly wrong, however, when so many people accept such a theory, true or not. The reverend may be correct when he says, "The main goal of education is for children to learn to become better citizens in society; that's the bottom line. . . I think this is an area where the New York City school system has failed."

HOPEFUL VOICES

The fact that there are successful students means that there are voices of hope. Both young people and their parents believe in education. Moreover, many parents must be successful in handing down these beliefs to their children. And many parents are happy with their children's school. Mrs. Robinson, a mother of four, one of them adopted, is a happy parent.

Interviewer: How is it working for the boys?
Mrs. Robinson: Well, this school in particular is great. I mean I think this is the only school I know in the Bronx that is really helping the kids learn better. They have more concern, more feelings; I mean they're wonderful. The other schools around in the area, they don't have no feelings for the kids, no consideration, they just don't care about the kids.

The Belief in Education

In spite of the failures of the school system, perceived or otherwise, in spite the fact that racism exists on the personal as well as the systemic level, in spite of the violence and the fear of violence, these parents see the value of education. They may complain but they come into the school buildings, talk to teachers, volunteer to help. Mrs. Patterson, who has been pushed and pushes back, demands the best for her children. Mrs. Rodriquez goes to meetings and participates in school-based management. "I feel that it is a good program because programs we didn't have before here, now they are here so it looks like there is hope for the school." The last two turns of the interview with the minister also end on a hopeful note.

Reverend: My emphasis is first on education and I want my kids to know that, because it is through education that we as minorities have climbed the social ladder. Since my children are minorities, there's no other way for them.
Interviewer: Yes, I think that knowledge is the only way we can make the change. If you want to grow up to be a decent human being, you have to realize it all begins with your education.

The Transmission of the Belief

It is not clear whether the parents of successful students have different beliefs about education than those of the less successful. It is not clear whether all the children of the parents in this chapter are successful. Neither is it clear that all successful students got their beliefs in education from their families. But it is probable that many of the parents of successful students have managed to transmit their beliefs to their children. Listening to Mrs. Samuels, below, I suggest that they transmit more by action than by words.

Mrs. Samuels: It has to start at home. The parent needs to get more involved in their children. They need to watch out for them, care about them, take them to school, pick them up from school. They should all do like that. I buy crepe paper and sparkles and make stuff like that. Let their minds start to create. Maybe it will push them more into wanting to be somebody, you know. Because I do as much as I can, I figure. I'm going to make me some cards for Christmas. I buy the stuff, you know, art stuff. And keep them out of the streets because there's nothing out there except a lot of drugs.

If they have transmitted positive beliefs, it is probable that they have also transmitted other beliefs as well: mistrust, fear, the hardness of life, cynicism. Children hear many voices; they experience many different beliefs, often coming from the same voices. Why do they internalize some and not others? The data we have here do not address this. They do not even give us much evidence that many of these parents function in happy families; they do not describe lives that seem particularly happy. But the fact that they have been interviewed indicates that they are on the educational scene; that they are involved in their children's schools whether they, themselves, are educated or not. Their children may not always like them being there but they are not simply offering lip service to some set of arbitary values which they do not really hold to.

Mrs. Patterson physically backs up her words. The minister was told by his interviewer that his remarks might get published and he openly suggests a racial conspiracy. If these parents are typical of those of successful students we can at least describe them as meaning what they say. That is what, I suggest, must be transmitted to their children. Whether they are actually egalitarian or authoritarian, nuturing or harsh—categories outlined in the previous chapter—cannot be determined from their voices. If nothing else, they are thoughtful and forceful. Perhaps these are the ingredients for the successful transmission of values.

THE PARENT SELF

Elsewhere (Farrell, 1990), in writing about teenage mothers, I suggested that a parent self sometimes develops in young people which encompasses all other selves. Among young people who have not developed student or career selves, becoming a parent—usually a mother—gives an identity. I suggested that if this is the only self they develop, however, they will not be very good parents. Since half of the respondents in this study were single parents, we can probably assume that some number were, at one time, teenage mothers. Among some of these respondents, being a parent is still probably the major part of their identities.

It should be asked whether the parents—who we can define as concerned activists—interviewed here have a more developed parent self than some others, particularly the ones they refer to in their criticisms. The few who were housewives and who seemed to be constantly in fear for their children certainly had an identity that revolved around being a parent. Obviously, we cannot have a definitive answer to this question with our data but we might further ask whether the parents of our respondents who were successful students saw parenting as their primary role.

Of course, we all know middle-class and affluent families where being a parent has become the raison d'être of adults, sometimes to the detriment of their children. Having been a special education teacher for nine years in an affluent community, I saw little correlation between weak or strong parental selves and children's problems, psychoanalytic theory notwithstanding. In the aggregate, there might well be a measurable correlation but in the context of the inner city, where there are so many other powerful variables like drugs and peer pressure, such a phenomenon as a developed parental self being used as an explanation of student success or nonsuccess would be simplistic.

In my previous study (Farrell, 1990), I described a household of a young man in a dropout prevention program and I suggested that the primary identity of his mother was that of being a parent. But having a strong parental self does not guarantee one's children's success in school nor does success in school imply that parents are more into being parents. Two successful students in the last chapter told of fathers who were "players," gamblers, and in trouble with criminal elements. Drugs were not mentioned but the use of addictive substances, of course, the most common criminal activity, can transform success to failure in both generations.

I will conclude by saying that these respondents in the chapter had strong parental selves. I cannot say how typical they are but their concerns, I believe, are typical. What parent in the inner city does not fear for her children, does not want the best for them? What minority group member believes there is no racism? And what parent who has no business to pass on to his sons, who has no estate to leave, who knows there is little monetary capital available for his offspring, does not want to invest in the human capital of education? To quote Tolstoy again, happy families—those who believe in something, who want the best for their children in spite of limited resources—are all alike.

6

The Student Self

Anthony's words started the introduction to this book. He and Orestes, who we will meet below, were each interviewed by different collaborators. Anthony, who has achieved a 92 percent average is exhuberant.

> Interviewer: Do you really like school or do you consider it something you have to do?
> Anthony: I love school and I don't care who hears this; I am in love with school because it gets what I want done fast.

Orestes, however, expresses a somewhat different attitude toward school.

> Interviewer: What do you expect? When you come to school each day what do you expect from your school and from your teachers?
> Orestes: What do I expect from my school? I expect it don't burn down. I expect to be taught a lesson.

Anthony and Orestes represent a range of attitudes and opinions that our respondents had about school. Anthony, we will see below, was not always so positive about school. He has the enthusiasm of a recent convert; in his case, his conversion was to education. The more matter-of-fact Orestes is also a believer. If he doesn't love school, he at least sees it as a means to an end. Orestes received most of his elementary education on the island of Jamaica in the West Indies where he thought that schooling was better. There was more discipline, he later said in the same interview. Although he aspires to be a doctor, he went on to say, he seems to have rather limited expectations of his secondary schooling in New York. But he believes his opportunities in the United States are better than in his native land and his future prospects, as far as he is concerned, outweigh any negative aspects of his current schooling. Even the exhuberant Anthony "loved" school primarily because of the perceived long-term rewards. Our respondents could be negative about school, about teachers, and about administrators but they all seemed to believe in the value of education in general.

BETWEEN SUCCESS AND FAILURE

Anthony and Orestes may represent somewhat different attitudes toward school among our respondents but they were closer than they were apart in these attitudes, at least as compared to at-risk students. Whatever their range of attitudes is, they both will probably go on to college. And although our respondents were all considered average or better students, they also demonstrated a wide range of academic achievement. In addition to this range of abilities, individual students might vary from year to year in their performance. Even Anthony who loves school and wants to be a psychologist has had his ups and downs.

> Interviewer: Was there ever a time when you messed up?
> Anthony: Yeah, when I was attending JFK before I switched to Norman Thomas, I went out with the wrong people and I started cutting a lot. I was going to none of my classes. Cutting is addictive, especially in Kennedy, so I broke out. I told myself I had to get out.

Even though our respondents are considered successful in school, that success does not come easily for many of them. But time and time again, they state that they take school very seriously and desperately want to do well. Perry illustrates this.

> Interviewer: What are some of the hardest problems you've ever faced in life?
> Perry: I think maybe failing, failing classes.
> Interviewer: And how do you deal with it?
> Perry: Oh, you mean how did I help myself? I went to extra help, studied harder, encouraged myself to do better.

That Perry's "hardest problems" have to do with failing classes demonstrates that he is indeed developing what we are calling a student self. Failing at being a student reflects, I suggest, on his sense of identity. Achieving a student self is not done without difficulty; many students don't always know how to go about accomplishing this. One young man discussed homework and studying with his ex-girlfriend. He is frustrated and angry but has not given up.

> Interviewer: What the hell's homework? I don't do homework.
> Roberta: That's bad, you know what I'm sayin'?
> Interviewer: I just, you know, like studying, I don't know how to study.
> Roberta: Me neither. If I have a test the night before, I just look everything over and, you know, if I don't remember that I keep writing it down so I remember.
> Interviewer: I don't write it down. I just read it, try to read it a couple of times and then I try to repeat it. I read everything from the heading down.

I repeat everything. But it's like hard because my sisters be running around the house: rah, rah.

Besides home life sometimes being difficult, school life can add greater problems to a young person's life. When asked how schools could be improved, a young man said, "I think if you took the drugs and the guns out and, um, and some of the clothing that people wear." The first thing a visitor sees upon entering a New York City school are security personnel with walkie-talkies. All visitors must sign in. I must always bring my City College ID. On the surface, students seem to take this in stride but being constantly reminded that schools can be dangerous places must take its effect even if the student himself has not been involved in unfortunate incidents. Because of this, we must ask whether a place where there are guns and drugs is a place for young people at all? It seems remarkable that any kind of a student self develops in any way in such environments.

Why is it that these students want to succeed in these places? I visit many city schools but my first reaction in many of them is to want to turn around and walk right back out again. They can be dreary, noisy, sterile, and/or dilapidated. This is, apparently, the reaction of many students as well. But our respondents tolerate it, apparently because of the perceived rewards. In a dropout prevention program at the City College, we found (Farrell, 1990) that less successful students still would like to graduate but they see a high school diploma as, at best, a credential. The students in this study look beyond a credential, not to a job, however, but to more education. They tolerate deplorable and disgraceful conditions because, like Orestes, they see school as a means to an end.

EDUCATION AND THE FUTURE

As we saw in chapter 1, our respondents, unlike their less successful peers, had definite ideas about their future careers. What we hear them saying here is that they see a definite link between education, though not necessarily high school, and career.

> Ginny: . . .so if I want to be an obstetrician, I can't just go to medical school without a diploma. . . .If I want to be that, I really have to work.

Most see school success as the only way to achieve success in later life. Peter, who we met in chapter 1, is an example of this.

> Interviewer: What are certain things that motivate you to do well in school and the con side of it: what are certain things that turn your mind away from school?
> Peter: Well, certain things that motivate me are: like I said, fear of becoming,

not a fear of becoming a nobody, but a fear of having to work those odd jobs with little pay, and little chance for improvement or moving up in the ladder or something or moving up in the corporation.

More of our respondents are women than men and Katie, below, sees success as a women's issue.

Interviewer: What motivates you into going to school?
Katie: Well, as I said before, I want to be successful. I want to have a means to support myself and be independent. I don't want to need a man to take care of me.

Katie was the only respondent who verbalized this sentiment although surely not the only one to be so motivated. Do these students stand apart from their less successful peers in their ability to link school and career success? According to our data, they do. At-risk students did not often verbalize making such a link but when a seventeen-year-old ninth grader is still in school after being retained in grade two or three times, he must be hoping for something; he must want to believe that schooling will somehow benefit him. If he drops out, of course, he might want to believe the opposite. Neither group, however, seems to see a direct link between the specific subjects they are studying (e.g., English, math, history) and the future. The successful students can see a link between education in general and future success. Success in school leads to more schooling which, in turn, leads to a successful career.

Another major difference in the student selves of the successful versus the less successful seems to be based on previous success in school. In spite of the difficulties they speak about, the students in this study have had more successes than failures in their school biographies. They have not been retained in grade; they have managed to catch themselves when they fall; they have not given up. Parents, teachers, and/or peers must have given them some reinforcement. They also have acquired more tool use, meaning, in this case, having more academic skills. Although I have no specific data on this, based on my experience as a teacher, I assume they read at a higher level and have higher level math skills. The at-risk students I studied may have had the potential to develop their academic skills but a few mentioned in their dialogues that they sometimes had to disguise their deficiencies. Because of all this, they, obviously, have different perceptions and attitudes toward school. These perceptions must both drive and be driven by their successes or lack thereof.

PERCEPTIONS OF SCHOOL

When we look at these students' comments about school, we see that they had much to say about teachers. To a lesser extent they spoke of the institutional environment, the social environment, but had very little to say about the content of their courses. Katie, who we met above, thought school was a means to become independent and therefore important to her life. But, except for the social environment, she does not voice enthusiasm about it.

> Interviewer: We're going to talk about your school. Do you like it?
> Katie: The school? The building I don't like. The people I love and the teachers are mediocre.

Katie's not untypical remarks address the institutional environment, the social environment, and her teachers. This section will address these three phenomena, along with course content.

Institutional Environment

The main complaints these students voice about school have to do with bureaucratic inefficiency and institutional rigidity. We will see in the next chapter that teachers have some of the same concerns. A typical example of the former is from a young woman in the tenth grade telling an interviewer, "I'm supposed to be in hygiene this semster and I'm still stuck in freshman gym. I don't know what's up." In the overall picture of urban education, this might not be considered a major problem. But one gets the impression from these dialogues, that the students do not have a sense of what institutional constraints exist untill they get tangled in them. They do not seem to get much help navigating the system. *The New York Times* (Lee, 1990, February 12) reports there are 1,000 students for every New York City public school guidance counselor. After being asked if she were passing all her subjects, a young Latino woman tells of a major decision in her education in which she had no input.

> Natalia: Um, barely passing French, slightly.
> Interviewer: Can't you drop it?
> Natalia: No.
> Interviewer: Why not?
> Natalia: Because all the other Spanish classes are filled and they don't want to transfer me and the lady herself doesn't want to change me; she doesn't want to lose another student. So I'm there for good and I wanted to drop her class for the spring term, but I found out that if you take a language at the beginning of the year, you have to take it for two terms and then your next year you can change to a different language, which is a real loss for me because right now I could be in Spanish 5. Then I could be taking my Regents. And instead I'm going to be taking a citywide test in French which I'm not really interested in. When you're interested in something you do good at it, but if you're not interested in it, it's not going to work out.
> Interviewer: Is there tutoring in that school?
> Natalia: Yes, there is. We have those homework helpers after school. We have whatever you can imagine there is.

Because of circumstances beyond her control, Natalia's grade point average will suffer. The "Regents" she refers to are statewide examinations that students take in a some number of subject areas in order to earn a kind of college prep diploma that is thought to have more prestige than a regular diploma. It is unique to New York State and while some might argue that it upholds "standards," it is a constant reminder to teachers that the state does not trust them to prepare their own final examinations. When I taught high school English in New Jersey one year, just a few minutes away from the city, I was making up my own finals while my colleagues in the city were prepping their students for the Regents. There is, of course, no evidence that the New Jersey students are any less prepared for college than their peers in New York. If anything, it is the other way around, at least when comparing suburban to urban students.

In New York City, it is these Regents examinations that drive the curriculum. On the elementary level, teaching styles as well as curriculum are driven by yearly systemwide tests as well. Phonics work sheets rather than whole books prevail in classes of young children. Certainly, as far as high school is concerned, one would think that teachers and students together might do a better job of deciding what to study. Common sense tells Natalia that one learns what one is interested in and enthused about. So, too, the material the teacher is the most interested in is what he does the best job of presenting. The Regents examination is another way of adding to the feelings of powerlessness that students like Natalia have and which, we will see in the next chapter, teachers have as well. Public alternative schools and private schools in the city don't require their students take these examinations and they seem to do better with graduation rates and college acceptances than the schools of our respondents.

Of course, there are positive factors about schools that students recognize. Natalia's mention of tutoring and "homework helpers" speak to programs set up by administrators and teachers within the schools that help students. Many students, like Anthony in the beginning of this chapter and like Lydia, below, have positive perceptions of school.

> Lydia: I'm saying once you get into high school you have to work hard, give some time to the books, but high school can be fun if you make it fun. I'm not saying once you get into high school it's not going to be boring. It's up to you to make it fun, but don't forget to study.

Lydia brings a positive attitude to school with her. Her mention of boredom, however, is a remarkable parallel to the perceptions of at-risk students in my previous study (Farrell, 1990). Boredom was the most common complaint of those students. Elsewhere, I have suggested boredom was a socially constructed phenomenon and not necessarily a reflection on the material or even the way the material was presented by teachers. I will refer to this in chapter 9. Boredom was one step in the progression toward dropping out and, for many students, being bored and letting your friends know was actually a form of resistance.

The students in this study accept that some methods and materials are boring but they tolerate it just as they tolerate other negative phenomena. Once again, Peter is another case in point.

> Interviewer: And things that turn your mind away from school. . . .
> Peter: Things that turn my mind away?
> Interviewer: So what are you telling me—that you like school all the time?
> Peter: No, I'm not saying that. I just like certain things about school but sometimes school is really kind of boring and repetitious.

The institutional environment of school, then, has both positive and negative elements. In summarizing all the data on institutional environment, we are led to believe that students, even successful students, at least verbalize more negative elements. Bureaucratic inefficiency, administrative rigidity, an ambience of boredom and repetition, and the specter of drugs and weapons are voiced more than school being fun, more than tutoring programs, more than helpful administrators or guidance counselors. Many of them seem to develop their student selves in spite of the institution.

Social Environment

Even if there were no compulsory education laws and in the absence of rewarding jobs, adolescents would at least, I suspect, show up at school on a daily basis more often than not. They might not learn anything, they might cut, they might not attend classes at all. But school is where the largest number of age peers can be found. In a dropout prevention program for high school students at City College, we were never successful at scheduling lunch activities. Not even college mentors, not much older than the high school students, were particularly welcomed at lunch. It was the time, the high school students stated, when they could talk with their friends. In spite of the perceived dangers, in spite of the institutional rigidity, in spite of boredom, school is a magnet. Unfortunately, we don't often capitalize on this.

We have discussed the peer self in chapter 3 and saw that this self is formed in school as well as out. The social environment of schools is largely formed by the peer selves of the students. Among our respondents, there were few complaints about this social atmosphere. When asked about the social climate, one young woman said, "It's good. Everybody gets along. There's no racial problem. There's a lot of white kids and Hispanic kids, a lot of black kids, and we all just hang out together and there's no problem."

Although racial incidents are made to appear to be on the upswing in our news media, they cannot be said to be common in the schools of New York and apparently not in the schools of our respondents. Of course, it must be remembered that in spite of the young woman's comment on race, New York is in large part a segregated school system. It might be argued that school population reflects neighborhoods but it is startling to observe the racial composition of northern urban schools almost forty years after Brown versus the Board of Education.

Perhaps we have forgotten the research of Kenneth B. Clark (1963) who showed us that black students in segregated schools were psychologically damaged simply by virtue of being in those schools. Clark's dramatic interviews of black children showing a preference for white over black dolls are now part of the lore of education and psychology. His research had a large part in driving the 1954 Supreme Court decision which, we all thought, changed the nature of public education in this country. It has not—at least not in our cities.

I was born and raised in New York, went to college there, and taught high school there as well, but left in 1969. In the 1960s I witnessed the efforts to integrate schools and the efforts to resist integration. Educational issues in the city at that time had to do with bussing and community control of schools. The times, they were a'changin'. After teaching in New England for fourteen years and getting my doctorate, I returned to New York in 1985 to work in my present job at the City College. When I first went out into the schools to supervise my field-work students, I found them more segregated than ever. In most schools around City College in Harlem, there is not a single white student. Jonathan Kozol (1991), in his startling new book cited in the last chapter, reminds us with his graphic descriptions and analyses of six different urban systems of the inequalities in our nation's educational system; separate is not equal.

Kozol (1991), using 1987 data, shows that many surburban school districts spent two to three times as much per pupil per year on education than do the cities they surround. Higher values on homes in the suburbs bring in more tax revenue for schools. In 1991, the pupil expenditures were higher but the spending imbalances were the same. More alarming is the fact that there are differentials between schools within the city. The tax rate is uniform in the city and school financing is systemwide. Kozol points out that schools in white neighborhoods are given more resources than those in black and Latino neighborhoods.

One would think that a simple central office reallocation of funds could change this. But Kozol (1991) has an even more devastating criticism. The inequality exists *within* individual districts. He compares in graphic detail two schools in the same district in the Bronx. In the black and Latino school, there is a much higher student-teacher ratio, far fewer computers and books per child, far less space, and absolutely dilapidated conditions. This is the situation that Mrs. Gifford mentioned in the last chapter. In the next chapter we will see teachers, *before* the publication of Kozol's book, making similar comments. Segregation and inequality have obviously become more institutionalized than ever in New York and, according to Kozol, in many urban school systems as well.

No one on the policy-making level in New York, as far as I can see, seems to acknowledge that segregation and inequality even exist, much less that there is anything wrong with it. Students don't seem to recognize or at least don't verbalize that they are segregated in school. The subtle effects of this, however, must impact on their psyches. They come to school for the social environment but, for many, like Anthony in his first high school at the beginning of this chapter, the social environment may be one of temptation to cut classes or demean school. Anthony had the will to change schools and build up his 92 percent average but like the fish who cannot know of the water he is swimming in, he and his peers may not see the insidious social environment that surrounds them, the social environment that segregates them and distributes support unequally. But on some level, they must realize that our society is not giving them their due. The interviewer below asked the same question to all her respondents; the answers were much the same.

> Interviewer: Do you feel that New York City schools are giving the best education possible?
> Ginny: I don't feel they're giving the education that they should because they're too big and they always cut the budget and taking back things and the teacher can only teach as much as they permit her.

Course Content

Conspicuous by its relative absence in the dialogues between these students is mention of academic courses and course content. Perhaps because I taught for so many years, when I meet a high school student I usually want to ask what he or she takes for courses. Algebra, world history, something new? Next, I am interested in what subjects he or she likes. As a teacher, I assume that interest in a subject usually makes for an intrinsic motivation. Although I usually get answers of some kind from those I ask, this line of inquiry is generally not a topic of talk among these students even when conversing in a school setting.

This is not to say that these students do not develop enthusiasms for subject matter. I do not recall sharing my passion for Shelly's "Ode to the West Wind" with any of my friends in high school. It took a few years of college with people of similar interests to make me willing to discuss literature in social situations. The social life of most urban high schools might not be conducive to academic discussions. The peer self and the student self may be only partially integrated in these students; they share common values about education if not common interests. Less successful students in our previous research, however, did not seem to share positive attitudes about education.

When there was talk of subject matter, it was always in the context of the teachers who taught it. In a dialogue in which an interviewer, after stating that English was her favorite subject, asked another student what subject she preferred, the answer involved a specific teacher.

> Sada: I never liked social studies or anything having to do with it. I hated social studies but now I have this teacher, Ms. Rosenfeld, and she's so understanding and she'll explain everything to you in such detail and she's really nice. I'm beginning to really like social studies.

Interviewer: That happened with me. This teacher makes social studies fun
in a way that you could never imagine. You can learn so much. . . .

Among these students, it appears to be that teachers and not subjects that are
a more important variable in motivation. Perhaps instead of asking a high school
student about his courses, I should ask him about his teachers. Any graduate
student knows that you pick your courses by the professors and not the subject
matter—unless a particular course is required. Perhaps we should not think
in terms of an *English* teacher or a *social studies* teacher but of a Ms. Rosenfeld
and people like her. Unfortunately, there were not many Ms. Rosenfelds
mentioned.

Teachers

If they said little about school subjects they had a great deal to say about their
teachers and about teaching in general. Most comments on how school should
be improved focus on teachers rather than administration or course content.
They praise some teachers; they are critical of others; they have thoughtful
comments on what a teacher should be and do. They seem to praise teachers
for competence and dedication. When asked what she expected from school,
Katrina gave an example of one good teacher.

Katrina: Well, see I have a couple of teachers that I really pay attention to
because they really teach you. Like several of my teachers, they say things
and it just goes from one ear to the other. Like my French teacher. He teaches
you and makes sure you have it in your brain. Then he reviews it until he
makes sure you have it. And if you have questions about it, he goes right
back to it until he makes sure you learn about it.

Natalia's voice, along with Anthony's, started this book. In this chapter she
complained of being stuck in a French class where she did not want to be but
seems quite pleased with the rest of her teachers. Moreover, she is able to take
their perspectives, something that never showed up in dialogues among at-risk
students.

Interviewer: How about the teachers?
Natalia: The teachers are really good. . .they are. Some teachers, you know,
they're human. Everybody has their bad days, but the majority of teachers
are really good, and if you need them anytime, free period, they give up their
free periods, which is good.
Interviewer: In my school. . .I like the school a lot. The teachers are real nice.
Of course, there are a few that have attitude problems here and they're. . . .But,
hey, nobody's perfect.

Boys who voiced critical sentiments tended to be concerned with the
instructional style of their teachers. Although Perry first mentions teachers'
respect for students as crucial, he then complains about style.

Interviewer: What are certain things that you expect to receive from your teachers. . . .

Perry: I expect respect just as I respect them. I expect a lot of things from teachers, but they don't give it to us.

Interviewer: Do you feel that as a New York City student that you're given the best education possible from qualified teachers?

Perry: I don't think so. I think the teachers are too rushy. They don't want to be patient. They don't want to be calm. Everything's too big and rushed.

Perry has a number of Regents classes. These, as discussed above, are necesarily test-driven. A certain amount of material must be covered in a certain amount of time. But Kent, another student from Jamaica, introduces another variable when he realizes that a teacher's style is based on his perception of students and that the ways teachers relate to students are also important.

Kent: Teachers should treat us more like people instead of machines to fill up. I think that would be a better way to help us learn.

Girls in general were especially more concerned with teachers' attitudes. Two Latinas spoke of what one perceived as a teacher's racism.

Interviewer: What do think about the teachers in your school?

Sada: They're nice but there's one teacher who sometimes gets on my nerves because he's a little racist. He likes to, if say, you answer a question incorrectly, he'll discourage you, instead of encouraging you. He'll make fun of you in front of the class and he'll tell you—Oh, come on, how dumb can you be?

Interviewer: It's not right for him to do that.

Sada: Yeah, it makes you nervous, like you said, they *de*-courage you, if that's a word.

Sada's creation and deconstruction of a word spoke to the attitudes of many of the young women in our data toward their teachers. From their remarks, they seemed to be more interested in the personal qualifications of teachers than in their instructional style and had opinions on what kinds of people teachers should be. Like Kent, they seemed more concerned with how teachers interacted with students rather than subject matter competency. They also wanted dedication and caring in their teachers.

Interviewer: What do you think teachers can do to make school more interesting?

Ginny: Um. They can teach us, in a way that we'll understand.

Interviewer: If you could decide what teachers are teaching, what kind of qualification would you install. . .?

Ginny: I think that instead of just hiring them because they have a qualification, they should also hire them because they show that they really, really want to do this and that they'll help no matter what. They'll help the student and they love what they're doing. Because some teachers do not like what they're doing and they don't care. . . .

Vanessa wanted teachers to loosen up and have a sense of humor and be conscious of what bores students. But, more importantly, she also speaks of what she thinks is the worst thing a teacher can do.

> Interviewer: Okay, let's get more into school, into the teachers, students, the attitudes, the surroundings; how do you feel? What kind of attitude do you think a teacher would have to stimulate the interest of his students?
> Vanessa: I think they should be able to get along with other people, have a sense of humor, and, you know make them feel, "I can be fun, but I can be serious." Some teachers don't bother to do that and they get straight to work and I really hate to say it, but it really bores the students. You don't want a bored student, you want one that can participate in class and the way to do that is to actually get along with them, to reach out to them and let them know that you're there. Cause everything's so crowded, you know, impersonal. So I definitely believe in a sense of humor, being there, letting them know definitely that you're there for them.
> Interviewer: And what do you think is the worst thing a teacher can do?
> Vanessa: To tell a student that they're a bad student, because I had that experience. My mother last year went to a parent-teacher conference and my history teacher told her I was a bad student.
> Interviewer: Did you agree with this or were you starting to believe this at any point?
> Vanessa: I was starting to believe it. . . .

SCHOOL AND THE STUDENT SELF

The student self, like the other selves we are discussing, is socially constructed. We saw in chapter 3 how peers help construct this self and in chapter 4 how the family could contribute to it as well. From our dialogues in this chapter, one thing we can see is that all these students valued education even if they did not particularly like school or individual classes. Roberta, in the first section of this chapter, told her ex-boyfriend that it was a bad thing that he was not doing homework. These students go to peer tutoring or take advantage of other help and even change schools if things are not going well academically. They actively seek out peers to help them construct their student selves. Most importantly, their career selves and student selves intersect and, in spite of often deplorable conditions, this intersection largely occurs in school if not because of school.

In chapter 1, I cited Jerome Kagan's (1984) analysis of the high status careers desired by young people and the difficulties these young people have achieving these careers. There are only enough of these careers for one-third of any age cohort. Kagan goes on to say that the young person's absolute level of skill is not as important as his position vis-à-vis his peers. It is in our system of formal education, notably high school and college, that the young person is classified into this relative position. If for no other reason, then, young people need school so they can compete for these positions. And in a competition, of course, there must be losers. In this study, we cannot tell anything about the absolute skill levels of these young people; we only know they do better than others. But, unfortunately, the development of the student self comes at the expense of their peers.

In dialogues among the at-risk, school was disparaged. The peer self conflicted with the student self. No one would admit to doing homework much less tell anyone else it was bad not to do it. Those students had a history of failure and, perhaps, "de-couragements" in their educations and by the time they got to high school they were in the wrong place at the wrong time of their lives. The students in the dialogues of this book were not in the best places for adolescents to be but they make the best of the only places that are available to them. The most succinct summation of the plight of the successful students was voiced by Donald.

Interviewer: Do you like school?
Donald: No, really no. But you need school.

If we could create places that they liked, where they learned for the sake of learning, we would be changing the school system and they would be able to change the world.

7

Interlude—The Voices of Teachers

After listening to the voices of young people as a way of looking into the student self and realizing that these voices often spoke about their teachers, it is reasonable to ask what teachers themselves think about their situation. In a separate study, as large as the one that forms the basis for this book, four colleagues and I were able to collect and analyze data to make some conclusions about inner-city teachers. From a research course I taught in 1989–90, I solicited four volunteers to be research assistants in a study of teacher attitudes. One was a junior high school teacher from Great Britain who had taught in China, one a junior high teacher from Argentina of Italian descent who was multilingual, one an American-born elementary teacher of Puerto Rican background, and one a Dominican-born elementary teacher. Both of the latter were bilingual and had been students in the city system. None had been teaching in the system for more than five years. They taught in four different schools, each in an inner-city area. The students in the schools of our respondents were, primarily, African-American and Latino.

Following the methodology of my two student studies, each collaborator used a tape recorder to interview fellow teachers who were involved with *both* successful and at-risk students. The term at-risk was defined, based on the collaborator's schools, as a student in an elementary or junior high school where fewer than 40% of its students read on or above grade level. Every year each school's aggregate test scores are published in the press and teachers are well aware of how their students compare with those in other schools. Although the results of standardized tests can be disputed, the scores contribute to how teachers *perceive* the relative accomplishments of their students and we are concerned here with teacher perceptions. High school data were not available and my collaborators used their judgments on whom to interview on that level.

Sixty-three dialogues were generated with sixty people from twelve schools. They ranged from first-year teachers to thirty-five–year veterans. Collaborative analysis of data yielded four major phenomena that teachers had to come to terms with: 1) the power structure of the schools, 2) parents, 3) colleagues, 4) students. The collaborators discussed these and discussions were recorded and transcribed as well. The material that is quoted was chosen because the four teachers thought it was essential for the understanding of their lives.

POWER AND POWERLESSNESS

Direct-Contact Administrators

Respondents categorized administrators into those they had personal contact with and those they did not. A new first-grade teacher from the Dominican Republic complained about her building administrators.

> I see the administration; they want them to be like soldiers. They have to be sitting there and you have to be in control and you have to be teaching them and I don't think it should be that way. That's the main source of stress for me as a new teacher.
> Collaborator: Yeah, and our principal didn't want teachers to mingle, she was very paranoid.

The pressure on teachers to have passive classrooms was not an uncommon research finding. Jane Carew and Sarah Lightfoot (1979) report this as well. Administrators and teachers, of course, often have different perceptions of the classroom and different ideas of what should be happening there. The collaborators of this study believe these kinds of stresses continue to fester and unless there is teacher-principal discourse, the stress will not be alleviated. Teachers can fall into a mode that is perceived as conspiratorial and reinforce what they see as paranoia.

A principal, however, can be seen as apart from the power structure. Teachers described some as very supportive and willing to ignore, if not oppose, "the bureaucracy." "My principal told me the board requirements were unimportant compared to what happens between the kids and me," reported a teacher in a school where only 32 percent of the students read at or above grade level. Administrators who have direct contact with teachers, therefore, can have a pivotal role. This is very much in keeping with the findings of Lightfoot (1983). At schools where teachers speak of being happy and fulfilled— "In spite of the problems, I really love it [teaching]; I would never give it up"— the principal is seen to be one of them rather than part of a power group. Unfortunately, not all the respondents spoke of such school situations.

"The Bureaucracy"

No one had a positive word for the administrators that teachers do not directly interact with. All spoke of massive amounts of paperwork. One teacher explained:

> I mean the bureaucracy, I mean getting through, uh, the bureaucracy, to a bunch, I don't know if it's paper or people....They make it difficult...it's

probably so simple to be a good teacher if you're dedicated and you want to be a good teacher and they make it hard to be a good teacher.

Sometimes the criticism was vehement. A seventh-grade teacher now working with gifted children but who had spent a hated two years in a low-ranking junior high described her situation.

I think it [the Board of Education] is a rotten institution that serves no purpose but pursuing self perpetuation. . .I used to see myself reacting to my own family more sharply as a sort of carryover. A built-in aggression. You are always confronting the world at school. You are always in a confrontational mode. Collaborator: Just living in this city keeps me in a confrontational mode.

The collaborator's comments, as part of the data, act as self-validation for both actors in the dialogue. The actors share values and a cultural content. Their shared perceptions of phenomena serve to socially construct those phenomena. The Board of Education which refers to the bureacracy as well as the elected officials has a shared meaning for teachers.

The main role of the board, as they see it, is the annual imposition of the standardized reading test, referred to above, that can determine whether students get promoted or not. In some eyes, this test also determines whether a teacher has been successful or whether a principal is running a good school. The board has other roles but teachers do not seem aware of them. In a later part of the above dialogue, the teacher's ideas are again validated by the collaborator who, in turn, has her reality reinforced.

Teacher: It's [the board] not lacking programs; it's lacking telling us of programs that are available to us.
Collaborator: You know, I'm totally ignorant of what they have to offer.

There are obviously creative administrators who develop programs, make innovations, and try to help teachers. But such help is often seen as an imposition and teachers construct a reality of the board for what it does not do. An elementary teacher, when asked about board programs, angrily responded, "We don't need programs; we need more Xerox paper." Near the end of an academic year it is not uncommon for a school to run out of supplies and the frustration this causes can outweigh any good the board does.

Another concern about the board has to do with school assignments. A teacher who is otherwise happy in his work voiced resentment and the feeling of utter powerlessness over a job requirement.

The idea of being told you have to stay in this district for five years once you are appointed, I think that goes back to servitude. You're locked into a job. I mean, um, you can go to the Board of Ed with your head bashed in and say, I want to get out of here because I've been beaten up so many times, I don't think you'd get anywhere.

Concerns like this might have to do with systemic structures rather than bureaucratic inefficiency. Teacher placement rules are usually union negotiated. Even with what is considered to be a strong union, many teachers do not feel they have the power to control their lives. One substitute teacher reported that the examination she needed to take in order to become a regular had not been given in three years. A teacher in an alternative school spoke of his old job where he taught five classes a day and had a homeroom, each with thirty-five students. "Nobody can deal with 180 humans a day," he declared. A female junior high teacher spoke of having no ceiling on the third floor of her school and where the water in the fountains was unfit to drink.

> You leave the system because the system itself doesn't help you. Systems are constructed to help people get things done. It seems to me that the system set up by the Board of Ed, the whole thing is set up to hinder and hurt the teacher, not to help her. . . . I never saw myself as a powerless person; I usually know how to get things fixed. Teaching has pulled the rug out from under me.

The teacher reality of powerlessness evoked here was not at all unexpected. Many teachers complain about administrators. The labor/management split often leads to an adversarial relationship in and out of education. But the vehemence of the criticism was unexpected. Few people made jokes or waxed philosophical about teaching conditions. The commonsense reality they describe seems to be the reality of a desperate situation and the forces that run the schools are seen as uncaring if not malevolent.

PARENTS

Lack of Parental Support

There was almost a universal teacher voice on parents. "Parents are the biggest problem," said a first-grade teacher. The teacher of the gifted, cited above, stated, "Parents are the main variable." A junior high teacher with thirty-five years experience said of the dropout problem, "*That*, I will have to lay at the door of the family." Teachers who so often take the brunt of the blame for school failure might, in turn, blame parents. It is important to note that this was not a case of one ethnic group blaming another; teachers of all ethnic groups described parents negatively.

A teacher from Cuba with twenty years experience attributes most problems in the schools to the recent influx of other Latino immigrants. He claims there is no parental supervision and that families are unstable and always moving from one school to another. Many parents, he says, "don't even bother to pick up their child's report card." He and our Dominican collaborator agreed about the harm done by other Dominican parents taking their children out of school for weeks at a time for family visits.

"Parents don't care" was a refrain that appeared many times in our data. Events like parents' meetings, our collaborators agreed, are notoriously poorly attended and this is interpreted as not caring. In chapter 5, we saw that some parents attribute this to fear. A Puerto Rican teacher with seventeen years in the same school makes contradictory statements. On one hand, he says parents are not available but that they pamper their children by buying expensive clothes and Nintendo games. While many teachers remark on the expense of such items as children's sneakers, it is impossible to know if children are overindulged. The same teacher later said that many parents never hug their children. While this is something he cannot know either, it is the reality he and many of his colleagues have constructed. Lightfoot (1983), on the contrary, found that teachers in her "good" high school that attracted inner-city students, which was also in New York, saw parents as allies. If parents are seen as not caring, teachers will make fewer attempts to contact them. If teachers make fewer attempts they will have less contact and parents will be seen as less caring.

Lack of Parental Competence

Many teachers spoke of reasons why parents do not support them and their reasons are often deficit theories. They frequently commented on the single-parent family and a lack of literacy among parents. Some mentioned parents not helping with homework but others spoke to parents being unable to help. One teacher spoke of a seventeen-year-old mother of a four-year-old daughter: "She was 13 when she had her." One of our collaborators, a junior high teacher, believes that the mother of one of her students was at the same level of maturity and had the same adolescent reality as her daughter.

Conflicting realities and lack of confidence can frustrate the desired parent-teacher partnership. A fourth-grade teacher tells of a dilemma.

> I thought anytime a child had a a problem you'd call the parents in and ask for help and talk about it. But what that does is focus on the child when the problems may well come from other problems in the family. I think it may do more harm than good sometimes to focus on the child and label the child as the problem when the problem might be the whole constellation of the family.

If parents are seen as unable to solve problems, teachers might well ignore those parents. So, too, if there are language barriers. Many of our respondents, however, spoke Spanish. But many of them claim that there is not a specific language problem but rather a language-in-general problem.

Language Deficit: Bernstein Revisited

A bilingual teacher in an elementary school started his dialogue with his observations over the past ten years.

The language skills that the children are bringing in either language. . .are very poor. . . .parents are not really speaking to their children. . . .their language experiences in Spanish as well as English are very limited.

Collaborator: Yes, parents are not speaking to their children because the simple things, a bat, the lid of a jar, they don't know what it is.

Teacher: Parents are talking to their children by saying "esto" [this], "aquello" [that] rather than actually labeling. Also, many parents speak to their children in a very condescending manner where all they do is really scold them or. . . .

Collaborator: Criticize them?

Teacher: Or talk with them in a very simplistic language.

This was not an uncommon observation among our respondents. The collaborator, who is also bilingual, is able to pick up the cues of her colleague and they mutually perpetuate their belief. This exchange recalls Basil Bernstein's (1970) controversial thesis on restricted versus elaborated codes. Bernstein argued that working-class parents in Great Britain tended to mainly use the restricted code when speaking to their children whereas the middle classes used both. Working-class speech, therefore, has a more restricted vocabularly and syntax. Working-class children, Bernstein claimed, have a smaller vocabulary than middle-class children.

Bernstein had many detractors and does not seem to be emphasized in teacher education programs. In any case, few respondents, we think, ever heard of him. It is noteworthy, therefore, that, due to their interactions with children, teachers have socially constructed, as seen in the previous dialogue, a deficit theory of language that emanates from parents. But whereas Bernstein saw language coding as functioning to maintain class boundaries, our respondents spoke to no social implications for the reality they have created. They did not see their conclusions as going above the family to the social system.

The Need to Educate and Mobilize

Although the teachers did not have many good things to say about parents, a few spoke to the needs of educating and mobilizing them. A Dominican second-grade bilingual teacher, a mother of three, spoke of empowering parents. When complaining about the deleterious effects of standardized tests, she alone commited herself to action.

I believe I will have serious problems in this school because if they tell me that my students are going to be holdovers I'm going to send the parents to the district office and I'm going to tell them to say that the teacher believes that their children are ready for promotion but the school administration does not believe so. I really don't care if they fire me.

COLLEAGUES

Our respondents seem to, in their words, "sink or swim" on their own without much help from anyone else and, surprisingly, not much communication with other teachers. Of course, the way a teacher's day is structured makes it difficult to interact with colleagues; there is little time for consultation. Only one respondent was involved with team teaching and the technique is, apparently, not promoted in the system. But a number reported working in a cooperative atmosphere. No one seemed to be critical of previous teachers although one can always blame children's inadequacies on previous instruction.

Only one respondent, a special education teacher, reported getting a great deal of help from colleagues and some were actually hindered by them. One dedicated young teacher arranged to have breakfast for her class and a neighboring teacher told her the group was making too much noise. A kindergarten teacher in a school where only 30 percent of the children read at grade level reported that another teacher asked her, "Why don't you just stay there and let them play all day?"

The latter comment was indicative of one of the most discussed phenomena of our respondents—teacher burnout. A high school teacher spoke of colleagues with twenty or thirty years experience to whom teaching is "just a job." A first-grade teacher sees others with ten or twelve years teaching who have no enthusiasm and are "just waiting to retire." Such "models" give a fifth year junior high teacher some anxiety.

> After your first year, in your second you get positive feedback. In the first year you're just giving and giving. In the second you start feeling more confident and you get back a lot of energy; it restores your faith in kidkind. Then maybe after twenty years it gets tiring, boring. I am enjoying it so far; I will keep on doing it till I stop enjoying it. I don't know how long that will be. There are teachers who don't enjoy it and they're a sorry sight. No drive, no fun at all. Kids are just annoying things that ruin their coffee breaks. They are depressing spectacles.

But no such teachers were interviewed. Our respondents, even those who had been teaching for years, did not manifest such symptoms in their talk. Perhaps the collaborators of this inquiry were not personally acquainted with burnt-out teachers or it may be, in face-to-face interactions, that teachers do not seem so afflicted or perhaps do not recognize their own afflictions. It may be that there is no such thing as a burnt-out teacher. Rather, some teachers may feel burnt out some of the time.

How much of teacher burnout is a socially constructed concept? Respondents in our dialogues spoke disdainfully of afflicted colleagues but such a syndrome may be a depressive reaction to the stresses of teaching that were alluded to by the same respondents. Because of the disdain, few such teachers would admit to being burnt-out, much less ask for support. We agree that burnt-out teachers exist; it is obvious that there is some percentage of bad teachers. How many there are is difficult to tell, using any research method, but they are part of the reality constructed here.

STUDENTS

Discipline

One area of agreement among our respondents is that children are too often out of control. Teachers who feel they have no power over their lives in school often feel they have no power over their students. There are tales of chaos, children screaming, and lack of implulse control among children of all ages. Elementary teachers complain that children come to them unprepared for school; secondary teachers claim that students are unprepared to go out into the world because of this lack of implulse control.

But they try to understand this lack of discipline. A third-grade bilingual teacher in a school where only 24.3 percent of children read at grade level explains one facet of the situation.

> They have no space to run around or anything so they just bump into each other and hit each other because that's the only thing that they see they can do. And the worst part is that we adults have accepted that as a natural way of interacting, socializing.

Indeed, elementary school teachers tended to be tolerant of noise and activity. "Students get very excited when they use hands-on materials and there is interaction between them and then they raise their voices and then the administrator says you have discipline problems." Another spoke of them "lighting up like Christmas trees" when they got excited. It would seem that discipline is often in the eye of the beholder; one teacher's chaos is another's excitement.

Junior high teachers more often spoke of chaos. Class control is a matter of survival. One teacher told of "whacky kids" and how hostile they were the day after report cards; "it is horrible when the group turns against you." But she too understands; in junior high, children become sexually active. "Sometimes you have to be a bit whacky. But, you know, when you realize these kids are jumping out of their skins because of their hormones." Although there is a great concern about lack of order, some appreciate the energy level. A new teacher who did not know what she would be teaching until the first day of school is gratified that she is never bored.

> Teacher: I had these awful secretarial jobs before, which are so boring.
> Collaborator: Are so boring. From the first five minutes that you go to the office and this is really....
> Teacher: That is the one thing I like about it.
> Collaborator: Combat zone.
> Teacher: Yeah, there is lots going on. And it *is* [a combat zone]. There *is* a lot of energy around. There is really; there is a lot of fun.

No research has ever suggested that teachers thrive on chaos. We do not think that is what is quite evoked here. For some, however, there is a satisfaction in thriving in spite of the chaos. Compare the satisfaction of people who work on the floor of the stock or commodities exchange. Being around energy invigorates many people. In spite of the stereotype of an "ideal" class where students are sitting quietly in rows and in spite of our respondents' complaints about chaos, it may be that not all teachers are gratified by peace and quiet. Neither, of course, are all students; both they and their teachers might need to be in high-energy environments.

But there is also a belief that "kids *want* discipline." One junior high teacher told of students absolutely ignoring his requests on the first day. Immediately after school, he went to a stationery store and bought a large, thick ruler. When a child ignores a request, he hits him on the leg. It was either this or quit teaching, he explained. The unexpected result was that he has become one of the most popular teachers in school. He claims that he does not "punish" anyone but that he "gets their attention." While we do not advocate his methods, he is probably right in his claim.

Ability

Elementary school teachers had somewhat different notions of their students' academic ability than did secondary teachers. Other investigators have found this over the years (Book and Freeman, 1986; Indire, 1969; Masling and Stern 1966). Our elementary teachers were more apt to feel their children are victimized by standardized tests and labeling. "The education system here is geared to the white middle class," says a Latino teacher. But "children can learn!" she declared. Others echoed this.

They are concerned with the social problems as much with the learning problems of their children. "We have to deal with medical problems, emotional problems, and family situations," said one elementary teacher. And although they understand, they are bothered by cultural differences. A first-grade but not first-generation Latino teacher in the same school lamented:

> Ask them about Robin Hood, you know, who's he? He was trying to do good for the poor, you know. Who's Cinderella? Who's Snow White? It's like gone. It's, it's incredible what they pick and what the parents choose to tell their children. . . .They don't want to talk to their children about Little Bo Peep and stories that were so. . .that were so innocent. . . .

Secondary teachers were more willing to verbalize about their students' lack of academic ability. "They are not the top," said a junior high teacher with thirty-five years of experience. But he goes on to say, "The student feels that if he sits in class he is entitled to pass whether he learns something or not. . . ." The same teacher also feels that students are being given the wrong messages.

I had one student today...saying, "I'm going to be a pediatrician." She can hardly read. They live in a fantasy world. Nobody corrects them. Everybody tells them they can be whatever they wish. But you can't! I couldn't be a nuclear scientist even if I wanted to because I do not have that kind of knowledge or that kind of ability. Things have to be kept in the proper perspective.

On the other hand, the teacher who complained of there being no ceiling on the third floor of her school bemoaned the fact that none of her students would attend Bronx High School of Science, an elite public school recognized as being one of the finest in the nation. "Nobody is going from here. That is a shame because there is certainly the talent. There is no ambition. Ambition is not something that comes and knocks you on the head."

A high school teacher said he saw little difference between special education students and those in the mainstream. But a junior high teacher stated, "Every kid is different." It did not seem, however, that many of our respondents had given up. Although there were comments that "some teachers don't like kids," such people were not encountered in our dialogues. In spite of the complaints, we thought that an overall positive feeling about students was verbalized. Teachers may need to see students as positive factors in their lives.

CONCLUSION: THE TEACHER SELF

Despite a prodigious amount of research on teachers, little is known that is generalizable about the characteristics and attitudes of those who work with inner-city students in a multicultural environment. Using an interpretive approach, teachers from within the setting of this inquiry gathered, reduced, and analyzed the collected data. It was decided to define and describe the major factors in the professional life of a teacher from teachers' points of view. These factors were the power structure, parents, colleagues, and students.

From our data, it can be seen that teachers feel beset by parents, administrators, and various facets of the system. Their criticism of administration echoes the findings of Carew and Lightfoot (1979) but the negative comments about parents was at odds with Lightfoot's (1983) description of school personnel mobilizing parents in what she defines as a "good" New York City school. One teacher reported that he had spent six hundred to eight hundred dollars of his own money on materials in his first year of teaching. He was beset but, obviously, dedicated. Many verbalized that they were not highly regarded as professionals but few verbalized negative feelings about themselves. Although they were negative about parents they were less so about students.

The plurality of subjective voices we heard leads us to agree with those researchers (J. W. Getzels and Phillip Jackson, 1963; Dan Lortie, 1975) who reported that there is no one kind of teacher self. We did, however, hear new voices that represent new populations of teachers. There were many black, both African-American and Caribbean, and many Latino voices. A Latino math teacher in a junior high bilingual program, speaking to a Latino collaborator, emphasized his commitment.

> For example, when I'm going to work in the morning; I live in New Jersey and work in the Bronx. When I'm driving in, in the morning, I think of the equations I will write on the board. I think about the color chalk I will use, the colors I will use on the graphs, what colors I will use for the answers, what type of problems I will introduce at the beginning so they will lead toward the solutions to more complicated problems to come. . . .That fascinates me. As long as it's in my area with bilinguals because they're our people, you understand?

This was one of the few dialogues that spoke to the presentation of subject matter. We believe that most of our respondents, like those of Blase (1986), are more concerned with "relational and counseling outcomes." And even for the teacher above, we believe, math was not primarily taught for its intrinsic value but because it can be a tool of empowerment. Embedded in our data, we think, because of the references to chaos and turmoil, is that teachers are, indeed, most often "caught up in the value of the moment" as was found by Jackson (1968) and Lortie (1975).

Our respondents, overall, spoke of themselves in a positive light. A junior high teacher with twenty-three years of experience gave an honest reflection when asked if he was happy or not.

> I have very good days and very bad days. I am extremely happy when a lesson is effective and I feel all the kids have learned some skill. But I'm such a bad class manager that I do not feel that I have. . . .Compared to my ideal image, I don't feel that I'm doing nearly what I could.

Some became angry but their anger seemed appropriate. One junior high school teacher blames the system.

> I was so angry at the end of last year, that I was participating in a system that said to these kids that it doesn't really matter at all what you do; you are going to fail here, and you are going out in the real world to fail, so who cares?

But for the most part, our respondents claimed to like their work. They feel "fulfilled," "satisfied," "very satisfied." "I've changed the kids; the kids have changed me," said a first-grade teacher. "I'm not moving," declared a special education teacher. "If you can make it teaching in New York, you can make it anywhere," offered an elementary teacher echoing a popular song. But none of these were naive; another special education teacher with eight-years of experience adds, "A good teacher will fight the system."

A commonsense question to ask, after reading this text, is can teachers continue functioning in the reality they describe if it remains unchanged? The total positive forces in their teaching lives must outweigh the total negative forces. If not, they must leave the profession or become cynical. Those who are positive may not continue to be so. If as many as 40 percent of students leave school before graduation in spite of the fact that there is no work for them, as often happens in the innercity, we cannot say the positive forces in the whole system outweigh the negative.

Teachers appear to be powerless; parents are powerless. Is it as bad as all that? A few of the respondents have been teaching for twenty and thirty years without, apparently, losing self-esteem or voicing cynicism. It seems unlikely that the teacher who spoke of having the rug pulled out from under her, the other who spoke of the Board of Education as being "rotten," the Dominican teacher who feels the stress of forcing her students to behave like soldiers can continue without losing some of their dedication, their creativity, their effectiveness.

Another commonsense question is why these teachers are so negative about parents. Lightfoot's (1983) respondents, as we said, were not. Surely, they are aware of the tremendous difficulties of the poor, the non-English-speaking, and the fearful in urban areas. One wonders if they have any idea of what their students' parents think of them. The public sees urban education as anything but successful. If teachers are not to blame, it must be the students, their parents, and/or the power structure. Blaming the ultimate victims, the children, makes the teacher's lot untenable. Ascribing the problem to language and cultural deficits allows for a cause without attributing specific personal blame to anyone.

Since the basic act in creating the reality of this inquiry was the dialogue, it would follow that one desired action would be for participants, readers, and researchers to continue to engage in dialogues. A difficulty here is that what the dialogues uncovered tends to hinder teacher-administrator and teacher-parent dialogue. There would be few smooth dialogues between teachers and a "rotten" administrative system or with "deficient" parents. In our "possible world" (see Tyler, 1986 in Introduction), anonymous voices engage in dialogues; in the "real" world of common sense, voices are people. Also, dialogues between people of unequal power can become the monologues of those who have the power.

A number of urban school systems are currently implementing school-based management plans to give decision-making power to both parents and teachers. Giving teachers voice is one step in empowerment; giving parents voice is another. Up to now, from the point of view of our respondents, these voices have not been talking to each other. Hopefully such dialogue—like that in our text—would have a therapeutic effect on school systems. But when these dialogues "work" (when they are symmetric, when each participant can anticipate the other), they must be based on shared values. School-based management must be socially constructed by the participants and not handed down from above.

Although there appeared to be collegiality in our dialogues there was no evidence, stated or embedded, of camaraderie. Teachers did not speak of helping each other much. Teaching for tests, the course concept, classroom space, and scheduling often weigh against everyday teacher dialogue. If the voices of teachers are not heard by parents and vice versa, it may be that they are not heard much be other teachers either. If some teachers want order in the schools at the expense of energy while others feed on energy at the expense of order, they must come to an accommodation in their dialogues.

What seems most problematical in the "possible world" we have constructed, however, are the teachers' attitudes toward their students. "Students *can* learn!" "I feel all the kids have learned some skill." Teachers speak of feeling "fulfilled." But, on the other hand, students have language deficits, are undisciplined and violent, can "turn against you." The "world" we have constructed does not seem "possible" unless we admit that teachers' attitudes toward students are mixed. One high school teacher after much complaining, said, "Don't get me wrong, I like my students. They like me." Professionals do not have mixed attitudes; human beings do.

It may also be that teachers have mixed feelings about themselves. If a large percentage of her students fail, has not the teacher failed also? The respondents in the dialogues all came from what some might consider "failing" schools. The schools in this study were partially selected on the basis of low reading scores. Far too many of the students who start these schools never graduate. Teachers can blame parents and the power structure. They can have mixed feelings about their students. But part of this must affect them. The only way to produce a positive teacher self, as we have suggested, is to expand dialogue among all groups, in spite of the difficulties, and change the power structure of school systems. Chapter 11 will speak to this.

8

The Affiliating Self

To the question of what one does after school, there were many different answers. "I go to a peer tutoring program, take classes for about an hour and a half." "I'm in the Dance Club." "My school has a Fashion Club." "I write for the school paper." "I go to El Puente" (community youth center). Moreover, they spoke very positively about these activities.

AFFILIATIONS

One phenonemon that characterized the students of this study whom we are calling academically successful was their participation in after-school activities. From the responses above, we can see that they spoke to belonging to school clubs and frequenting after-school centers. We will also see that they attended church and participated in church youth groups. They can be characterized, I would say, as joiners. A constant complaint voiced by social critics, commentators, and young people themselves is that there is little for high school students to do after school that does not require the spending of money. My students at the City College who, themselves, were successful high school students voice this as well. I do not have data to compare the number of social and recreational activities available in the communities of this inner-city population to, say, those of suburban or other more affluent communities but, if there are few such opportunities for recreation, the young people of this study seem to be able to find them.

The less successful students in my previous study, on the contrary, rarely mentioned belonging to groups or participating in extracurricular activities. Neither did they ever mention belonging to gangs and, in fact, as mentioned in chapter 3, gangs and street gang activity have declined in New York over the last twenty years. From their remarks, I would characterize those students as nonjoiners. But it was not as if they were socially isolated; there was a great deal of peer interaction and peer activity. One gets the impression, in fact, that they were actually more involved with their peers than are these more successful students. What they did not tend to do was engage in activities that were organized and run by adults. Their group, or what I call their outreaching or affiliating selves, were well developed but were developed in a different way from those of the young people of this study. They tended not to affiliate with organized groups.

I use the term "affiliating self" to generalize about a number of selves. When I was a member of the track team in high school, one of my most important selves was my self-as-runner. As a high school teacher I knew students who became enamored with computers and, although they did not verbalize it as such, they surely had developed a "self-as-hacker." A person may have a Baptist self, a Republican party self, an Elks Club self, etc., depending on his amount of involvement in these activities. And while my Elks Club self might not be seen to have the import of my sexual or career selves in the formation of my identity, what underlies my joining the Elks Club might. I might have a need to be part of something beyond my family and immediate friends.

Extracurricular Activities

Academically successful high school students are more likely to participate in extracurricular activities, especially nonathletic activities, than their less successful peers. They may be motivated by interest in the specific activity, by a desire to live up to or project a certain image, by a need for more social contacts, by a calculated attempt to improve their chances for college admissions, or by any combination of these factors. Eckert (1989) investigated the social class structure of a Michigan high school and found the not now unfamiliar categories of "jocks" and "burnouts." Jocks generally come from the middle class and they more often participate in extracurricular activities; burnouts generally come from the working class and do not so participate. They apparently do not feel particularly welcome in these activities. Although the social class distinctions may not be as great in the inner-city high schools of our respondents as in suburbs, the differences still may reflect class values and class expectations.

Extracurricular activities are largely adult-directed. Students who engage in them are more likely to have accepted various adult and societal values. The more they participate, the greater the variety of adult voices they hear and the more the values of these voices are reinforced. In recent years, because of budgetary limitations, there have been fewer and fewer extracurricular activities offered in the New York City school system. Such activities have become a limited resource. The norm in a well-funded suburban school might be that students are expected to participate in these activities. The norm in these inner-city schools is that they do not. The minority of students who do participate might be considered elitists or nerds by a number of their peers. If nothing else, they are "different."

Athletes, however, are not put down, especially in the inner city. But there was only one athlete in our sample and only in one other dialogue was an athlete mentioned. The former is a young woman we will learn of in the next chapter; the latter was mentioned by Rosie, the young woman we met in chapter 2 who complained that people only referred to her as "Bill's girl." Bill was captain of the baseball team. Being an athlete brings peer respect; joining clubs does not. . .except from fellow club members and teachers. This is especially true for young men but even young women can have a problem with this. Yvonne El-Amin (1992), a former student of mine at the City College, writes of an incident with four young women who were her "homies" in a New York junior high school but whom she later wanted only to avoid.

> It was only last summer that these four ladies jumped and beat up Maryanne because they were jealous of her receiving the part of Cinderella in the community play. When Maryanne's mother tried to stop it, her face was cut three times across her right jaw.

These attitudes need not be the prevailing ones in inner-city schools. Just a few blocks away from the City College in Harlem, is Junior High School 43 where only 38 percent of the students read at or above grade level. The school has a chess club which has come to national prominence by winning competitions over teams from schools with many more resources. The club gives all the students in the school a great sense of pride. This success was accomplished largely by the efforts of one very dedicated teacher. Without this teacher it surely could not have happened. Of necessity, then, extracurricular activities must usually be adult-directed. The students who participate are buying into someone else's value system and, as we might expect, are internalizing those values.

Those who do buy in tend to be the academically successful students. That is not to say that academic success precedes this kind of participation. Every high school teacher can tell stories of young people who have been "turned around" by getting "turned on" to some specific interest. Computers, chess, dance, music, journalism, sports, and cheerleading are some of these. Other than the instrinsic interest a student might have in these activities, participation in them gives recognition even if only by a very small group and usually by a teacher. So of course, part of the recognition comes from adults. Students who are characterized as joiners may have already internalized certain societal values or they may begin to internalize those values by joining something.

But in one interviewer's high school, there were some after school clubs whose value some of our respondents questioned; these were clubs or school organizations for students of specific ethnic groups.

> Interviewer: What do think of these clubs. . .like, you know, black groups, Italian groups? Doesn't that separate people?
> Laurie: I don't know, it keeps them off the street.

At the City College, there is a Black Students' Association, a Dominican Students' Association, and an Italian Students' Association. We saw in chapter 6 that, in at least one of the schools where this study was conducted, there were no racial or ethnic conflicts. But ethnic pride is very conspicuous in New York. Ethnic groups have associations, parades, festivals, and are very much part of the political life of the city. Ethnic pride does not necessarily translate to ethnic conflict or even separation.

Our data indicate that there are sometimes ad hoc extracurricular activities which are established and maintained by students themselves within the schools. I know of one Bible study group, for instance. And Joe, whom we met above telling of peer tutoring, is training to be a lifeguard with two of his friends.

> Interviewer: You mention that you do activities, after school activities.
> Joe: After tutoring, I go to relax to get the classes off my mind. And my school has a swimming pool. And I just go into the swimming pool and let out my tension by swimming and I do a couple of laps, like maybe twenty laps.

Community Centers

New York City has comunity centers, youth centers, church centers and other similar social agencies. Both the at-risk students and the students of this study were aware of these and both groups participated in them. Young people will go to places where there are other young people. One particular center was mentioned by ten of respondents of this study; it is called El Puente (The Bridge). Because of its name, it tends to attract Latino students but, of course, all are welcome. The students who did speak of it, seemed very knowledgeable about what it had to offer. The young people in my previous study did not appear to be as involved with the centers they knew about as did these ten people.

El Puente offers cultural clubs, sports, Outward Bound, photography, piano instruction, aerobics, English as a second language classes, and many other activities. One of the young people interviewed had gone on a trip to Russia through El Puente. It would seem that a center with such a rich variety of activities would attract large numbers of young people. Yet some are obviously more involved than others. Some are more ready and willing to take advantage of the opportunities offered. Perhaps there is a social milieu about such centers that attracts some young people more than others. Perhaps a student who has not achieved much success in the world of adults, as exemplified by school, is less willing to believe that he has a chance to go to Russia, or learn to play the piano, or even learn English very well.

Aerobic classes and trips to Russia are for the middle class, or those who aspire to the middle class. And although, as I have stated, the concept of social class did not often come up in our data, I believe young people are aware of it on some level. Fine (1991), in an analysis of autobiographies of sixteen students who appeared to be successful in school, found that they had achieved some degree of class consciousness. She suggests that the main criterion that students used to classify themselves, however, was not income. She cites Pierre Bourdieu's (1986) concept of "cultural capital" as the main criterion. Among Fine's respondents, cultural capital included a family whose basic needs were being met, who had higher aspirations, who believed in education, and who lived in a decent neighborhood. A selfconsciousness based on aspirations brings to mind Markus and Nurius's (1986) concept of "Possible Selves" that will discussed in chapter 10.

Fine's astute analysis helps explain the young people of this study who see the offerings at El Puente as opportunities and who believe they will benefit from them. They have some amount of cultural capital and, even though they may not be consciously aware of it, their actions and affiliations at El Puente will tend to increase this kind of capital. If you participate in middle-class activities like aerobics classes and world travel, you are middle class or, at least, on the way towards it. The affiliating self (e.g., hacker self, Baptist self) seeks the other selves it wants to be with. But the "cool" student and the homeboy may not want to become affiliated with young people who are buying into a value system that, through the agency of school, is rejecting them.

Church Groups

A surprising number of the young people in this study spoke of belonging to church groups, especially youth groups. When I taught a class of students in a dropout prevention program we had set up at the City College, only one of them attended church regularly and only because he was forced to by his parents. However, the great variety of social services provided by churches and religious organizations in New York are essential to the life of the city. Churches, for example, feed a large proportion of the homeless population. Government agencies in an era of declining tax revenues could not carry out this task alone. Many churches run their own schools and in New York there is a large Catholic school system. But they also contribute to the community, although to a lesser extent, by establishing after-school centers and youth groups. Although many adolescents would scoff at the idea of attending a church-sponsored group, a number of the young people among our respondents attend and join such groups.

Some of them are strongly involved with the sponsoring church but others simply attend because their friends do. Such a group gives them another social outlet. A student of mine at the City College has a fairly well paid part-time job teaching physical education in a church-sponsored after-school center. He got the job because of his affiliation with the sponsoring church. Being part of a church-sponsored youth group also gives a young person access to help when it is needed. This help can include counseling, family intervention, and various other social services. It is one more connection that the affiliating self makes.

But is church more than simply a social group? The access to help and social services referred to above can probably be found at El Puente, for instance.

The social life that a church youth group provides might seem rather unexciting compared to, say, the image of "good times" in TV commercials, let alone "real life" where sex, drugs, and rock 'n roll are all readily available. Some of the comments of our respondents suggest that they see something more than social gratification in their religious affiliations. This is something not often discussed in research on inner-city adolescents. Some of them lead me to believe that there is another self which may be considered a subpart of the affiliating self but which may also be a distinct socially constructed self in its own right and which may come into conflict with other selves or be successfully integrated into the young person's identity.

THE SPIRITUAL SELF

Gloria seems to be speaking of another kind of self when asked about her religious beliefs.

> Interviewer: Okay, do you believe in God?
> Gloria: Yeah.
> Interviewer: Of what faith do you belong?
> Gloria: Christian.
> Interviewer: Do you believe that your faith plays a big part in your life?
> Gloria: Yeah, my faith—it kind of motivates me to have faith in myself and other people. It helps build up, give determination to do things.
> Interviewer: Do you go to church regularly?
> Gloria: Yeah.
> Interviewer: Do you think that religion should play a greater part in our government?
> Gloria: Yeah, they should pray because it helps a lot.

Twenty-eight of the young people interviewed spoke of being active churchgoers. All of these were Christian. One was a member of the African Methodist Episcopal Church; one spoke of being nondenominational; three were Catholics; ten were professed Christians but their specific denomination was not stated except that at least one belonged to a religion that emphasizes the conversion experience (see below under "Pentecostalism"); twelve were Pentecostal. This is not to say that the other young people were not churchgoers; the subject simply did not come up in the interviews. Because the sample may seem skewed in favor of Pentecostals, especially when we would expect many more Catholics with the substantial Latino population here, it should be pointed out that one of the interviewers was a member of a Pentecostal church and she interviewed many of her friends.

The Orthodox and the Unorthodox

Oscar states he is a Christian and appears to be a member of a conversion religion. I would guess he is either a Baptist or a member of a Pentecostal church. When his interviewer asks him to explain his religion to her he recites his own kind of creed which is ingenuous, elegent in its way, but also quite orthodox.

> Oscar: Well, way back in the days. . .God sent his son which is Christ—we are not sure if it's December 25th so we just celebrate Christmas on that date— but He sent His son and He grew up and He was on Earth for a purpose—to die for us, to set us free from sin, sin which is bad stuff. And, um, when He died and was raised and all of that and to be a Christian you have to accept Christ, which is when you ask Him to come into your life and ask Him to wash away your sins and keep the faith and grow in the word.
> Interviewer: Do you believe that your faith plays a great part in your life?
> Oscar: Yeah. Why? Because if I don't have Christ, if I don't pray, I don't feel comfortable and, you know, God is a protector and when I go out on the street I want to be sure that someone is protecting me, or someone is there and Christ is there.

Oscar knows what he believes and seems to have a basic but not unsophisticated understanding of Christianity. His religion has a great deal of personal meaning for him and gives him emotional comfort on the mean streets of the city. He does not come across as holier than thou, is not preachy, and he seems able to integrate his religion into his everyday life.

None of the young women interviewed offered such a defined picture of what they believe. Natalie, however, constructs her own religion when she tells her interviewer, who is obviously a close friend, how her concept of the Deity has influenced her life.

> Natalie: God has gotten us closer. That's how She's influenced me.
> Interviewer: God?
> Natalie: I believe God has put you in my path, even when we were little. We're very close and we can relate to a lot of things. We understand each other, a lot, and that's good too.

Perhaps some young women are less willing to accept the stereotypes of religion and more willing to reconstruct it. In so doing they might be better able tolerate inconsistency and therefore may appear less orthodox. In a conversation that started out about sex and not religion, a young woman who stated that abortion should be permitted was asked if she believed in God.

> Cissie: I believe in God. Yeah, I believe in God. I believe in God. I believe that there's a Jesus and there's the saints and I believe in the Bible.
> Interviewer: What religion or faith do you belong?
> Cissie: I'm Catholic.

Many Catholics, of course, are more accepting of abortion than are their church's hierarchy. Many of the young people here have apparently thought about religious issues and are willing to discuss them. This was not the case for the at-risk students in my previous study.

Religious Controversy

School prayer is an often hotly debated issue on the American educational scene. Unlike many other controversial issues in education, its effects cannot be measured nor does anyone argue that they can be measured. It is not like the debate between teaching of reading by phonics or by whole language methods. It appears to be a purely ideological issue but not even the religious students among our respondents seem emotional about it. To a student who thinks religion should play a greater part in government, an interviewer poses a question.

> Interviewer: But there is also something else to think about. I'm going to play someone on the other side. If we were to choose a religion to make a religion play a bigger part in our government—what part would it play? Would there be prayer in the Senate or something? What kind of part would religion play because they want prayer in the schools. How do you feel about that?
> Gerry: I feel that's okay.
> Interviewer: But also which prayer would we use? Because when they're talking about prayer in school they are talking about making one prayer. . .everybody recite this prayer. It's also to think about what prayer to use. Could we use a Muslim prayer? If we use the Muslims', Christians are going to be upset. If we use the Christians', certain types of Christian workers in another organization would get upset. It's hard to think which religion would become the primary religion in the U.S., don't you agree?

Prayer in the schools is not an emotional issue in New York. Condom distribution is. We saw in chapter 2 that students tended to think this was at least a practical idea. One young man who is a Pentecostal Christian and stated he was a virgin was not opposed to condom distribution. "I think schools should. Parents won't and it can save lives," he responded to an interviewer's question on the subject. Even though he practices sexual abstinence, he is in touch with the reality of adolescent life and does not believe he should try to inflict his views on anyone else.

Gerry's interviewer, above, who seemed to question prayer in schools was a Pentecostal Christian. Both she and the young man who took the practical view that condom distribution could save lives do not seem to fit the popular conception of this branch of Christianity. Even though many of our respondents are religious people and seem to have developed something we can call a spriutal self, they are not rigid about it. A number believe that the Deity actively influences their lives and can even be feminine. One can be a Catholic and favor abortion. Although they believe the Deity may actively affect their lives, the contested religious issues of the day may not. When they do, these young people more often come down on the side of practicality and reason.

Pentecostalism

Does the fact that Pentecostalism is the modal religion of this group of young people affect our data? Just what is Pentecostalism anyway? In the minds of many people it includes Holy Rollers, snake handlers, and Jimmy Swaggert. Even some of our respondents have a stereotypical concept of it.

> Interviewer: Do you believe in God?
>
> Jeanne: Yeah, every Friday night I go to a youth group meeting where we talk about God and we learn more. I mean we have to become more stronger in my faith. But yeah.
>
> Interviewer: But what faith do you belong to?
>
> Jeanne: I'm Christian...
>
> Interviewer: [I'm] Pentecostal.
>
> Jeanne: Pentecost....Isn't that? In the ninth grade this lady went really Pentecostal. The first couple of months I knew her she wouldn't wear pants or anything.
>
> Interviewer: That's certain parts of Pentecostals. Certain of them believe you're not supposed to wear pants or makeup and stuff like. My church isn't like that.
>
> Jeanne: No? She don't paint her nails. She don't wear makeup. She doesn't even celebrate Halloween. She says that if you have kids don't let them go out to trick or treat or anything like that. Are you...that into it?
>
> Interviewer: Well, in my family at least, my church at least, they don't say anything. Certain Pentecostal churches you have to wear a hat and all that stuff. In my church they don't. As long as you come to church, they don't care what you do to your hair, your nails or anything like that so, you know, it's not really that bad off.

In 1983–84, I conducted an ethnography of a Pentecostal church in the Boston area (Farrell, 1986). Pentecostalism had its origins in the United States during the early part of the twentieth century among people of generally lower socioeconomic status as a reaction to mainstream Protestant formalism. Its adherents are usually fundamentalist Christians whose religious services are characterized by spontaneity of worship rather than by learned ritual. Next to Catholicism, Pentecostalism is the most prevalent religion among Latinos.

Becoming part of the church is described in the *Tenets of Faith of the Assembly of God Churches* (1934), the largest Pentecostal denomination, as a two-step process. The first step, a conversion experience, is variously described by members as being "born again," as "committing one's life to Christ," or by "giving oneself to Jesus." This is an inner experience which most often involves repentence of one's sins and a lifelong commitment. This first step is taken by both adult converts and people raised in the church. The age that one does this varies but, in the Boston church where I carried out my participant observation, it tended to happen in adolescence, at least for those adolescents who remained in the church. All who have this experience may become members of the church simply on their word.

The second step in this process is the Baptism of the Holy Ghost. This has its antecendents in the historical [sic] event that Christians call "Pentecost." On the Jewish feast of that name, fifty days after Passover (hence, Pentecost), the disciples of Jesus, after He had finally left them, met together in a room and had a profound, collective religious experience which, apparently, galvanized them to preach all over the Roman world and establish the Christian church. The *Tenets of Faith* state:

> All believers are entitled to and should ardently expect and earnestly seek the promise of the Father, the Baptism of the Holy Ghost and fire....This experience is distinct from and subsequent to the experience of the new birth. With the Baptism of the Holy Ghost comes such experiences as an overflowing fullness of the Spirit, a deepened reverence for God and dedication to His work, and a more active love for Christ....The baptism of believers in the Holy Ghost is witnessed by the initial physical sign of speaking with other tongues as the Spirit of God gives them utterance. (p. 3)

This "speaking in tongues" or, more formally, glossalalia, being the most salient of Pentecostal phenomena, has been much investigated in the past. The stereotype that Jeanne, above, offers casts Pentecostals as participating in strange behaviors. To an observer of glossalalia, the speaker appears to lapse into an ecstatic state and utter meaningless syllables. But Virginia Hine (1969) summarizes, I think, the dominant research opinion when she says Pentecostals appear to be "normally adjusted and productive members of society." She suggests a functional interpretation of Pentecostal phenomena, when she states that "it [glossalalia] operates in social change, facilitating the spread of the Pentecostal movement affecting nearly every denomination within organized Christianity, and in personal change, providing powerful motivation for attitudinal and behavioral changes in the direction of group ideals" (p. 224).

The Pentecostals among our respondents, then, have undergone religious experiences, perhaps ecstatic ones, but these experiences enable them to affiliate with their church, with their social group, and, seemingly, with those who value education and assimilation into the greater society. Benjamin Beit-Hallahimi (1973), an Israeli social psychologist whose wide-ranging and insightful research includes both religion and minority adolescents, interprets "being filled with the Holy Spirit" as "being filled with the group spirit" (p. 227). Berger and Luckmann (1967) maintain that the conversion experience is "nothing much" in itself. The important thing is to maintain the belief system and, for this, one needs a "religious community." When Saul was converted on the road to Damascus, he adopted the identity of Paul but he could not remain Paul, they maintain, without the "Christian community" (p. 158).

Although many people can legitimately say that they have nothing that could be called a "spiritual self," other people do. Whether religious experience is socially constructed or whether there is a transcendental element in it cannot be determined here, if anywhere. To William James (1902), of course, in his *The Varieties of Religious Experience*, if they believe there is, there is. And, we must realize, it is very possible that one might have a spritual self in one point of her life and not in another. Religion can give these young people solace when they need it and a sense of acceptance and belonging.

COMMUNITIES WITHIN COMMUNITIES

Many people think of inner-city youth as being part of a marginal population and of minorities as being "outsiders." But rather than being "outsiders" these young people may be the ultimate "insiders." The spiritual self constructed by these Pentecostal students may be the epitome of the affiliating self. We have seen that the young people in this study are closer to their families than were students classified as at-risk. They are discriminating about their peers, often taking friends only from specific communities, only from those who aspire to professional careers, only from those who affiliate with the same clubs, community centers, and churches. Whereas the at-risk students affiliated with groups of friends, these students affiliate with larger groups and with peers only so far as they are also affiliated with those larger groups. Moreover, the larger groups are not generally groups of their own making. These are already existing groups, set up by others who represent the adult world, the body politic, and, if you like, the establishment.

Fine, cited above, distinguished successful from unsuccessful students who she called, respectively, "graduates" and "dropouts" (Fine, 1991; Fine and Rosenberg, 1983) by attributing to dropouts a "communalistic orientation to their relation with kin and community" but to graduates an orientation to their "sharing families" but with that sharing ending "at the boundaries of extended kin, not into the community." She further attributes to the graduates an orientation that "distinguishes firmly 'us' from 'them' " (1991, p. 135).

While it is apparent that the successful students in the current study do indeed distinguish us from them—an attitude endemic to those who join clubs and seek select affiliations—it was not apparent from my previous study that any of the at-risk students had a community orientation. In fact, I would predict that in the future these successful students will have a far greater community orientation than will the at-risk I previously studied. The fact that they are more willing to join already existing groups and that they affiliate with institutions like churches points to a greater likelihood of more affiliations in the future. In the African-American community, churches are often the driving forces behind community organization. It is well known that political success in this community most often begins in the churches, a fact that even white office seekers recognize. Today, in both the African-American and the Latino community, it is members of the middle class that provide leadership.

For a brief time, notably in the 1960s, that was some degree of radicalization of members of the lower classes and the lumpen proletariat, even of those who had spent time in prison. Groups like the Black Panthers organized communities and often provided services like breakfast programs for children. This no longer seems to be the case and even those former radicals who are still involved in community organization or politics have become members of the middle class and take part in conventional political activity. It is difficult to forsee the at-risk students of my previous study developing the type of political consciousness that leads to creating and joining organizations. The young people in this study, however, have already developed patterns of affiliation. It is from people like them, I suggest, that future community leaders will arise, although their affiliating selves and academic success will not guarantee them access to positions of leadership or financial success in a society that has not come to terms with the racially based systemic inequality that we discussed in chapter 6 (Kozol, 1991).

The affiliating self, as I said above, might be generated from a need to be part of something beyond one's immediate family or friends. It may be an interim self or a series of interim selves—the chess player self becoming the school newspaper self becoming the class president self—in the socialization process leading to an identification with the larger community. In order to feel part of larger, more remote, communities beyond the family—the city, state, and nation—one might first have to feel part of a smaller, more intimate community. The chess club, the school newspaper, the school, the youth group, the comunity center, the church might serve as these more intimate communities. One must be trained to be a citizen.

Does this mean that the loner, the student who chooses not to join anything, will have a more difficult time becoming a citizen? Not necessarily, but it would seem that many young people are alienated from school and marginalized by society. An artist or an intellectual can tolerate marginalization. A young person with no marketable skills, no history of success, and insufficient social skills to become part of organizations cannot. He will seek friends who are also marginalized and, at best, develop a counterculture. The young people of this study have some awareness that they are in the margins but strive to move toward the middle; they need to believe they will be accepted by already existing groups in the greater society. Having a history of acceptance in more imtimate communities obviously gives them an advantage over those who have no such history.

Because of their affiliations, these young people listen to a greater variety of voices, acquire more knowledge about the adult world, gain more confidence that they can survive in that world, and engage in something that they enjoy with people who are or who will become their friends. But their affiliating selves look beyond their immediate friends. It is also easier to integrate their affiliating selves with their other selves. Parents are more approving of their children attending school activities than of hanging out with friends. Teachers approve of students in extracurricular activities. Almost everybody approves of young people going to church. Their student selves, their family selves, and their affiliating selves are integrated. And, as I suggested above, the development of their affiliating selves gives them an advantage in their quest to become integrated into the larger society.

9
Will—A Student Theory of Success

Susan, a young woman who described herself as half Italian and half Puerto Rican, when asked what she would do if she were to find herself failing, replied that she would go to tutoring and added, "tutoring is on your own will."

> Interviewer: I guess so.
> Susan: Because I don't think anybody's slow in this world. I mean people, if you don't mind me saying so, people think just because you're black, Hispanic, you'll never amount to anything in this world, but I think that's the biggest crock of bull I've ever heard in my life. Excuse the expression. I've seen a lot of Puerto Ricans in this world that from scratch amounted to big-time people—no drugs, no alcohol, but working and sweating their butts off every day in school.

When doing interpretive research, one tries to construct theory out of the data, in this case out of the words of the respondents. At the very least, a theory of success should answer questions from the actors' points of view (Erickson, 1986). In the dialogue above, Susan, by discounting that anybody is "slow," states her belief that "will," in the sense of "perseverance," is more important than "intelligence" and, as we will see, her peers seem to support this and have made it a part of the lore of school success. Because of the peer agreement, we must investigate the concept. However, it must be realized that there are other factors, as well, that contribute to success.

CONSTELLATIONS OF SUCCESS

The purpose of this study is to see what accounts for the success of these students relative to others who live in the same environments and attend the same schools. Obviously, there must be constellations of factors that account for success and such constellations vary from individual to individual. From the voices of these students in the preceeding chapters, it would seem that family relationships, supportive peers, and the perceived link between education and future success must be factors in these constellations. Good teachers and good schools should also be considered but they were not often specifically identified or much commented on by the students.

Family Relationships

As we have seen in chapter 4, our respondents, by and large, reported having supportive families and good relationships with their parents and siblings. These are obviously factors in their success but it may also be that their school success was a causal factor of smooth family interaction. We have also seen in chapter 5—as I have found in at-risk students (Farrell, 1990)—that virtually all parents want their children to succeed in school. A supportive family can be an anchor of stability especially when combined with supportive peers and the belief that there is a link between school and future success.

Supportive Peers

Chapter 3 pointed out the importance of friends in these young people's lives. If your friends and your parents have the same values, you do not have the kinds of conflicts described in chapter 6 such as whether or not to cut school or engage in other such behaviors. Supportive peers with positive values toward school, however, would not seem to be enough to insure success; your friends do not generally affect your physical well-being or give you unconditional love. But, of course, being able to integrate the family and the peer selves also contributes toward establishing an identity.

Education and Future Success

Even if a young person has the previous two factors going for her, school will seem like a waste of time unless it is meaningful. The ultimate meaning of school to adolescents must be the belief that it will lead to future success, as we saw in chapter 1. If there were no relationship between school and the future, students would do well to quit as soon as possible. But even young people who are doing poorly will at least voice a belief that success in school is linked with later success. Therefore, the belief alone is not always enough.

Intelligence

One factor *not* addressed in these data is that of intelligence. A commonsense explanation of success may be that the respondents in this study are simply smarter. But let us point out again that our respondents were not considered "gifted" and were not in one of New York's elite schools. The ability to graduate high school, which was how we identified the students to be interviewed, cannot be beyond the range of most young people. If it were, as I stated in the Introduction, there would not be a dropout "problem"; dropping out would be more expected.

Howard Gardner's (1983) now famous theory of multiple intelligences defines *an* intelligence as "the ability to solve problems or create products that are valued in one or more cultures" (p. 5). This, I suggest, should be the definition that teachers use when talking about what it is that underlies academic success. It is more meaningful than the concept of intelligence as a measurable quantity in each individual that predicts success in school, if not in life. The work of Stephen J. Gould (1981) refutes the notion that "intelligence" is a primal phenomenon that we each have a certain amount of. Such global intelligence does not seem to exist as a psychological entity but, according to Gould, is an abstract concept that has been reified by statistical analyses.

Gardner (1983) suggests that there are at least hundreds of intelligences and identifies and analyzes seven of these that he is careful to call "fictions. . .for discussing processes and abilities. . ." (p. 70). His partial list of "fictions" include linguistic, musical, logical-mathematical, spatial, bodily kinesthetic, interpersonal, and intrapersonal intelligences. Formal education in Western culture, by and large, emphasizes the linguistic and the logical-mathematical. Those students who have certain bents and, even to some extent, certain innate abilities—Mozart could not have come into the world a tabula rasa—will do better in our schools *as they are constituted* than others with different bents and abilities. But a general intelligence in terms of "who is smarter" or of IQ does not, I think, seem to be a factor of success.

In addition, none of the students suggested intelligence as a factor. Susan, whose words began this chapter, did not think that, "anybody's slow in this world." And Susan, I suggest, is well aware that there are special students who need special programs. Some are slower than others in some areas. In the Introduction of this book, I mentioned my former student, Dale, the mentally retarded young man who managed to graduate high school. Dale did better than other mentally retarded students I knew (and some mainstreamed students) because he developed a work ethic; Dale could be counted on to do the job he said he would do. He had the tenacity to do so.

WILL

Data to Theory

If there was one explanation that pervaded the data, although not asked as a specific question, it had to do with volition. Embedded in the data cited in this study were such comments as those of Anthony in chapter 6 who told himself he had to change schools; or Christian in chapter 3 who realized she had to pick her own friends; or Peter in chapter 6 who had to make himself overcome boredom. Some used the word "will"; some "willpower"; others "motivation"; still others had no word at all.

> Jeremy: Well, you see, I think that if you really want to learn, you learn. But if you really want to be an outsider and just hang out with your friends then that's what you do and that's what Bushwick [High School] is basically known

for: its violence and the people who graduate. But if you believe and put your mind into studying and to try hard to succeed in life.

In accounting for success, they seem to be pointing toward something irreducible and self-driving, something not easily attributable to anything else.

> Interviewer: What is the main thing that affects your schoolwork? I mean what is the one thing that determines whether you do good or bad in school?
> Vinnie: If I feel I can do it.
> Interviewer: And where do you get this motivation?
> Vinnie: Well, I don't think anyone else can have the motivation for you because if you don't have it to begin with, then no one can really change your attitude about it.

Because the term "motivation" is strongly linked to attribution theory by many psychologists and educators and because there is a myriad of research (including my own doctoral dissertation) that looks at motivation as attribution, I prefer the word "will" to describe the success factor referred to by these young people.

> Interviewer: So that's kind of. . .will that some people have. I still don't understand why some people have willpower, have strong willpower but they just let their peers take over or whatever. . . .

Will is what is operating, I believe, in the following actual case. A particular student tells of playing a sport after school and then just getting home in time for supper. After supper, she talks on the phone with friends for two hours and then is so tired that she goes to bed. In this, she seems to be a normal, if not studious, adolescent. Sports can fill a student's afternoon. Talking on the phone to friends is an extremely important part of a high school student's life; she needs social contacts other than her teammates and each of her afternoons are filled. And, again, sports are tiring.

But then she matter-of-factly says that she makes herself get up at 4:00 A.M. to do her homework. This, I suggest, is what distinguishes her from many other students who attend school, play sports, have a normal family life, and socialize on the telephone. Apparently, no one wakes her up at four in the morning; she does that completely on her own. I cannot think of another way to describe what she does or another phenomenon to attribute her behavior to, that is more appropriate than the word will. Will, as an explanation of success in the minds of these students, is what, as we will see in the next chapter, Jerome Bruner (1990) calls "folk psychology." As such, it should not be ignored.

The word will has not generally been used by psychologists and educators in recent years. Bruner (1990) suggests that psychologists in the positivist vein are uncomfortable with "intentional-state notions as belief, desire, intention"— and I will add, *will*—"as explanations" (p. 15). Other objections to the concept of will may be due, at least in part, to the unfortunate prominence of the term in the pseudophilosophy of National Socialism in Germany before and during World War II. Previous to that, Nietzsche's use of the word in his critique of Judeo-Christian morality, particularly when he afforded it precedence over reason, gave it over to extremists of various stripes. The rise of stimulus-response theory and, more specifically, behaviorism as the dominant psychological schools in the United States in the 1950s and 1960s left no room for the concept of will. A person could be motivated by his reinforcements but will was relegated, along with mind, self, and soul, to mythology and poetry.

Social psychological tradition, however, in the United States has recognized something other than a stimulus-response theory of motivation and volition. George Herbert Mead (1934) spoke to man's ability to select the stimuli he needs to maintain what he called the life-process. Although he does not use our term, his notion of *selection*, in this case, can refer to will. Tamotsu Shibutani (1961) writes of the importance of different people in the same environment performing for different audiences (and, I would add, with their different selves) when he tries to explain motivation. This leads to the work of a major thinker that Mead, who died in 1931, could not have known of and to whom Shibutani had only limited access.

Vygotsky and the Problem of Will

Lev Semonovich Vygotsky (1987), the Soviet psychologist who Bruner (1986) calls one of the three (along with Freud and Piaget) "titans of developmental theory" (p. 136) lectured on the "problem" of will some sixty years ago. Bruner (1987) suggests that Vygotsky was a cultural theorist as well as a psychologist who described man as "an expression of human culture" (p. 1); man, therefore, cannot be analyzed alone. His lecture on will had not been translated into English before 1987 and, with the deemphasis of the construct of will, Vygotsky's effort was neglected.

After having presented a picture of the lives of our respondents, I would like to adapt Vygotsky's already existing theory to frame and fortify the emic theory or lore of our respondents and to partially explain academic success in the inner city and anywhere else, for that matter. I do not think that the respondents' explanations, as stated, offer sufficient data on which to build a "grounded" theory (see Glaser and Strauss, 1967, cited in Appendix) which answers the questions of this inquiry. They seem to be groping for a primal theory of will in their inability to explain where it comes from. But if we reject a primal theory of intelligence, we cannot do otherwise with will.

According to Alexander Luria (1987), a student and later co-worker of Vygotsky and who introduced his ideas to the United States, his compatriot's theory rejected: an autonomous (primal or spiritual) theory of will, an associationist (e.g., attribution) theory, and a theory based on affect. He posited a developmental and structural-functional paradigm of will which, although incomplete, gives us a theory that might contribute to explaining the success of the students in our data pool. It is based on the internalization of socially transmitted meaning to one's actions.

Vygotsky (1987) uses a mechanism identified by the neurologist, Kurt Goldstein, to illustrate the development of will in the child. This is the mechanism by which a subject cannot carry out one set of verbal instructions to achieve a desired end—even though he has the ability to succeed in that end—but can successfully use another set. Such results, say Vygotsky, indicate the great significance of the external speech one hears in one's volitional actions.

To apply this mechanism to both successful and unsuccessful high school students, we can assume that both have heard the message that graduation from high school will lead to greater success. The respondents in this study certainly voice that sentiment. In structured intake interviews of students in a dropout prevention program at City College, *all* respondents—even seventeen-year-old ninth graders—expressed a desire to graduate and the belief that graduation would help them in life (Farrell, 1990). As I stated above, I believe that virtually all students have the intellectual ability to pass enough courses to graduate.

On the one hand, then, they believe the voices that speak to the benefits of academic success and, on the other, they have the ability to achieve some degree of that success. Between the two separate structures of belief and ability is what Vygotsky calls "will." Will, to Vygotsky, is an auxiliary complex structure that connects the other two separate structures. When this auxiliary structure is less developed—as in the cases of many students—academic achievement is elusive. Their abilities remain dormant, at least in the situations they find themselves, for example, school.

How then does the will develop? According to Vygotsky (1987), "The development of a child's will begins with primitive voluntary movements [in infancy], then moves on to verbal instruction, and is completed with the emergence of complex volitional actions." The "primitive voluntary movements" represent the child, to some extent, "applying modes of action to himself that were previously applied to him by adults." He then must internalize the verbal instruction until there develop "structures in which the individual listens to himself when he is speaking and carries out his own instructions" (p. 357).

Will, it then follows, is developed by internalizing the voices one hears. If one only hears one set of voices espousing one set of values, only one set will be internalized.

> Interviewer: So why do you think kids are messing up these days. What kind of structure do you think they need to get that motivation that you have? Anthony: In my words, I think they need someone to idealize. Like someone their age to idealize. They need....What's really messing them up is peer pressure. They don't have correct choice in friends because, um, my friends, the ones I chose before I really messed up. That's when I think I really learned how to choose my friends because they didn't really help me much in school at all.

What is notable about our respondents, as pointed out in chapter 8, is their involvement with extracurricular and organized extraschool activities especially as compared to our previously studied at-risk students. The former hear voices from many different sources—family, pastors, teachers in nonteaching roles, youth workers, and, most of all, peers who listen to and believe the same voices. The latter often hear voices exclusively of their peers; from parents and teachers they only get what we referred to in the Introduction as "the speech" (see Farrell, 1990, pp. 63–64) which they disregard.

Will, then, is a socially constructed phenomenon that becomes internalized to one degree or another and is conceptualized here, in both the voices and the minds of the subjects of this study, on what Berger and Luckmann (1967) call "a pretheoretical level of consciousness" (p. 89). The young people in our dialogues have not, by and large, developed a theory of will to the point of verbalization. Their voices reflect those they have heard and continue to hear. Obviously, there is a direct relationship between the development of will and the social networks the individual creates or finds herself in.

A word of caution should be said on the dangers of reification here. We have seen how Gould (1981) refutes the notion of intelligence as a reified statistical abstraction. Erikson (1963) points out that "ego," the basis for his theories, is not an entity but a principle of organization. Berger and Luckmann (1967) do an analysis of the concept of reification as a corrective to what they consider the reifying propensities of theoretical thought. Reification is dangerous because it involves the apprehension of phenomena [like will] "*as if* they were something else than human products—such as facts of nature, results of cosmic laws, or manifestations of divine will" (p. 89). Will is a construct used here to summarize and conceptualize what these young people say. Vygotsky's similar construct with the same name is used to give them credence.

In my previous work, I have been critical of such things as celebrities doing TV spots imploring youth to stay in school and political figures urging more foreign languages, more algebra, and more Shakespeare to improve education. The implied message is, all you need is will. By so doing, they put the onus on youth rather than on the educational system or society at large to improve; such systemic improvement, after all, might necessarily entail an increase in public funding. Urgings like these and the implied messages reduce education to a form of cheerleading. Individual will (a.k.a. guts) was what I relied on as a track coach to develop talent and win meets. The ability to run fast and the perseverance to develop that talent, however, is not often generalizable and does not necessarily transfer to success in school nor, of course, in life.

It should be pointed out, moreover, that will, even as a process, may not be a generalizable psychological phenomenon. Gardner's (1983) theory of multiple intelligences, to again make the parallel, suggests there are, rather than one generalizable phenomenon called intelligence, a set of abilities such as logical mathematical, verbal, spatial, etc., intelligence*s*. Perhaps, too, there are different kinds of wills. The will to succeed in school might be different than the will to create rap poems or to succeed on a job. Many people have dropped out of school, of course, and gone on to become very successful with careers, families, and life.

The factors in the constellations mentioned at the beginning of this chapter that contribute to school success: family relationships, supportive peers, the perceived link between education and future success, as well as caring teachers, contact with other adults, and previous success to build on, all may drive or be driven by what we call will. Psychological factors such as intelligences, impulse control, trauma effects might also override, underride, or be part of such constellations. Will, however, should not be seen as one other *factor* in the varying constellations of success; it is rather, as defined by Vygotsky, a *process*.

In an interpretive study, we must give emphasis to the concerns of the actors even if these concerns are embedded in the data rather than stated explicitly and here they are both. Hence, the emphasis on will in this chapter. Furthermore, using the concept of will gives us a vantage point to connect the individual with social phenomena, the psychological with the sociocultural. Also, that will is developmental means that it can be strengthened, as a process, and that situations can be created that aid its growth.

A further point: Vygotsky's concept of will need not be taken in the elitist sense of who's smarter, who's got more willpower? The teacher in chapter 7 who complained that, although there was talent in the junior high school she taught in, there was little ambition, was using the word ambition like the young people in this study are using the word will. If we try to make will a quantifiable phenomenon as many psychologists and educators have tried to do with intelligence, it will be of no more use to us than scores of standardized tests are in solving the problems of inner-city education. Will, in that sense, can only become part of one of the deficit theories: "They just don't have the intelligence"; "They just don't have the self-esteem"; "They just don't have the will."

The socioeconomic circumstances of the lives of the young people in this study are not much different from those of their less successful peers. They live in the same neighborhoods and attend the same schools. That they believe they have more will to succeed in school does not mean they are better than their peers; it means that, although they may have heard the same voices, they were in particular circumstances within their environments where their peers, teachers, parents, and/or other adults reinforced the internalization of those voices.

BREAKING THE WILL

Schools and Teachers

Our voices, the voices of educators, are what we would like students to internalize in the development of the will to succeed in school. But what is it that they hear in our voices? Because a number of the undergraduate courses I teach have fieldwork components, I visit five to ten classrooms a week. One of these was a racially mixed fourth-grade class which had a white female teacher. I could not help but notice Bobby, an African-American boy who never seemed to be doing his assigned work. Moreover, he was scolded by the teacher at least once every time I was there. Bobby reacted to these scoldings with what I would decribe as a surly look and a mumbled comment. How much of his teacher's scolding voice, I wondered, could he internalize?

Now I do not mean to infer that this woman was a bad teacher. She seemed to do fairly well with the rest of the class and I judged that there was learning going on. Nor am I implying that the mode of interaction between the teacher and the student was determined by race. Each of the scoldings appeared to be for legitimate reasons, at least from the teacher's point of view. The boy was out of his seat, was not working, was doodling, was talking with another student, was throwing something. I am sure that the teacher would maintain that she was scolding behaviors and not the boy.

But there was no single behavior, as far as I could see, that, if it were isolated, would not be ignored. Therefore, another student could commit the very same offense and not be scolded. I cannot believe that, on some level, this does not go unnoticed by Bobby. Nor do I think that Bobby keeps a tally of his unacceptable behaviors vis-à-vis other children but, on some level, he is likely to interpret his scoldings as being unfair in light of the other children not always being scolded for the same indiscretions he commits. He might also interpret his scoldings as being racially based. But this is speculative; what I do know is that he did not enjoy school and did not seem to have a will to succeed in that environment.

And what about young people who are not scolded but who are unable to finish task after task? Or those who complete tasks and yet fail test after test? A hard-working teacher may dutifully correct a student's written assignment with numerous detailed comments on the returned paper. Those of us who write would dearly love to have such a critic before we send out our work to be judged. But the student who gets a paper back that is literally covered with red marks has been judged and may not be able to see the bloody criticism on his paper as very constructive. To constantly see his inadequacies pointed out to him may break his will to write better papers.

Even if a teacher is careful not to taint a student with an image of failure, even if a teacher is forgiving of mistakes, incorrect answers and incomplete work can be destructive of will. Creating products or solving problems (e.g., algebra word problems) is essential if a student is to discover intrinsic rewards of academic tasks themselves. A teacher may have praised his student's efforts to the heavens but if she cannot find correct answers on her own she may be unable to transform, in Vygotsky's words, "the meaningless situation into one that had a clear meaning" (p. 356). This transformation is effected, according to Vygotsky, by the same mechanism—which is to say, process—that he defines as will.

Peers

If what we are calling will is developed by internalizing the voices one hears, do they not hear conflicting voices?

> Kathy: See, my mother, my mother encourages me into doing things, but you she's old fashioned. She's not modern like nowadays. She thinks everything is bad. Going dancing is not right. If you talk to too many guys on the phone, it's not right. She is very old fashioned. But in this school and high school, there's more friends that have more, they think more and they have more experience and they know what's right and what's wrong and they will tell you what's best.

Parents, of course, have always seemed hopelessly old fashioned, at least from their children's point of view. Now it may be possible that Kathy is right about her mother. But she seems to have rejected her mother's voice completely in favor of those of her peers. We do not know what decisions she has made in choosing her friends but it was the sole reliance on friends' opinions that characterized many of the at-risk students in my previous study. I suggest that the greater variety of voices that young people hear, the greater the chance that they will internalize those voices.

Private schools, parochial schools, and boarding schools seek to limit the variety of voices that students hear. In this, they are often successful and their students seem to have a desire to achieve. Of course, these schools also have the option of removing those students who do not internalize the voices and do not develop a will to succeed. But such schools, on some level of understanding, apparently recognize the power of peer voices. In this investigation, we are looking for what is *in* students to make them succeed but we must remember that what we are calling will is still a socially constructed phenomenon.

What I believe is that the will to succeed in school among many inner-city adolescents has been broken. It is quite probable that this may even have occurred before they arrived in secondary school. I have suggested elsewhere and in previous chapters of this book that many inner-city students are unable to integrate their conflicting selves into an identity. Their peer selves seemed to be their most developed selves and, in light of Vygotsky's (1987) concept of the development of will, I now suggest that this results in them hearing fewer voices from fewer different sources.

STRENGTHENING THE WILL

If will develops, as Vygotsky theorizes, are there ways of fostering this development? I think so; will, as we define it, is not a primal phenomenon. In the final chapter of this book, I will suggest having smaller classes in smaller schools with a maximum of flexibility as a way of improving education. But as far as what happens *in* the classroom, all students have similar needs: they need to have school tasks appropriate to their abilities; they need to complete those tasks and see their finished products; they need to see sufficient meaning and have sufficient interest in their tasks to want to engage in them. If their school tasks were to meet these criteria, I believe they would have the will they need such that the construct might not even be mentioned by them in these dialogues.

The students in this book who achieve are driven by a belief that academic success is important to future happiness but some, like Natalia in chapter 6 who is trapped in French, do not always have appropriate tasks or meaningful tasks. Passing French will be an act of will. For many, a grade on a Regents examination is the closest they can come to seeing their finished products. Not seeing any intrinsic interest in their subjects, they look for general strategies to help them, for example, techniques how to study and the will to put them to use. But if they were interested, if they had appropriate tasks, if they could realize finished products, they would not need general study techniques. They might have to learn the technique to solve an algebra problem or the technique to make a mortise and tenon but they would not need to find a magical general technique of studying school material. As it is, without interesting, appropriate, and doable tasks, they tend to attribute the ability to study to a primal kind of will.

> Interviewer: Do you have a special study technique?
> Carla: Well, I have my little techniques, but I think the best way to study is just to let your mind know that you are going to do something; that you are going to pass this test.

Compare the dialogue above with that in chapter 6 in which Roberta is talking with her ex-boyfriend and they mutually admit that they do not know how to study. Perhaps what they are saying is that they have found nothing they want to study.

Most importantly, however, to strengthen their wills, they must "practice" using them. Since volition is the act of willing and choosing, students must have the power to make real choices. If there is to be a will to achieve in school, students must have real choices there. Simply hearing the right voices is not enough. I can tell my students anything but if I don't trust them to act on what I say, I can never say my voice contributed to the development of their wills. In the final chapter, I will describe schools where students have real choices over their education and, in fact, over their daily lives in those schools.

The classroom suggestions outlined above, where and when implemented, could help insure that the wills of students are not broken. But will is largely developed, according to Vygotsky, from the voices one hears. Therefore, a concerted effort should also be made, it seems to me, by both schools and extraschool agencies, backed by financial and other support from the greater society, to increase the number of extracurricular and extraschool groups and activities available to young people, as discussed in chapter 8. Young people need to hear a variety of voices that strengthen the link between education and the world of work; they need to have peers who hear and believe those voices as well. Moreover, they need to hear those voices, I believe, in situations where they are not captive audiences as they are in most classrooms.

Such suggestions almost seem like platitudes but we saw in chapter 8 that these recommended activities have been on the decline in urban areas often because of reduced funding for education. Other factors also contribute to this. During the 1990–91 basketball season in New York City, one public high school, because of unruly student behavior, took the incredible step of eliminating spectators from games. Two basketball teams and a cheerleading squad for each played out their games in a locked gymnasium. Now many who have taught in inner-city schools might see the justification for this but it obviously defeats the whole purpose of a sports program. The vast majority of inner-city students, as we have seen, already do not participate in extracurricular activities.

Since there is no dearth of physical energy among adolescents, one would think that there would be an abundance of outlets for this energy. The number one "sport" at the University of California, San Diego, is considered intramurals. Unorganized playground basketball in New York City is of the caliber of many colleges. Smaller schools, in my experience, have easier times setting up intramural programs, clubs, and other activities although they may not have competitive varsity sports. Such activities are not costly. Youth programs in community agencies are not costly either, in themselves, but these agencies suffer with the decline of public funding even more than do schools.

WILL AND BOREDOM

Among at-risk students in my previous study (Farrell, 1990), the word most used to characterize school was "boring." Classes that I heard on tape recorders that seemed extremely interesting to me were described by my student-collaborators as "boring," "the boringest," "the most boring." On further examination, boring classes had some similar characteristics. Very often they began with the teacher returning papers, questioning students about assignments not done, and otherwise setting up a judgmental situation. Students characterized classes as interesting when they had a personal liking for the teacher and did not see him or her as judging them. They distinguished "boring" from "good" classes on the process rather than the content of teaching.

Boredom also seemed to be a socially constructed phenomenon. If your peers thought a class was boring, you tended to describe it that way. There were even physical signals as to when a class was boring. Students would put their heads down on their desks in actual or feigned sleep in such classes. Many teachers, incredibly, tolerated such behavior even when half the class appeared to be dozing. I speculated that dozing might be an unconscious form of resistance to school. Boredom was part of a socially constructed reality in which school had little value.

What of students who recognize the value of schooling and higher education? Are they ever bored? Looking back on Peter's remarks in chapter 6, they are. "I just like certain things about school but sometimes school is really kind of boring and repititious. You just have to make yoursef do it." Donnie has similiar notions.

Interviewer: What turns your mind off of school?
Donnie: Generally, I wouldn't say the teachers. Probably the students. Sometimes it can get distracting, going to class. The teachers are boring sometimes.

The answer to whether good students are ever bored is obviously yes. But, for them, boredom and its effects are not signs of resistance. Even under the conditions I outlined above, some necessary work is tedious. At those times, the socially constructed phenomenon of boredom is overcome by the socially constructed phenomenon of will. You tolerate the boredom in order to develop needed skills.

While teaching mathematics I sometimes ran into junior or senior high school students who did not know times tables. Because of that, they were totally stymied in learning any math at their grade level. I implored them, I threatened them. I drilled them, I played math games with them, I put them on programmed instruction. They did not appear to have any learning handicap that would prevent them from learning times tables and I say this having been a certified learning disabilities teacher. But, by the time I got them, they had been "learning" times tables for ten years and they were completely and utterly bored. In the end, unless you are blessed with an eidetic memory, you learn times tables the way you become a good quarter miler. You run until you are tired and then you run some more. And then you practice it again and again. To many, there is a satisfaction in that but the process is not always pleasant.

The will to learn times tables had collapsed in these young people. For them, boredom was the opposite of will; it set in when will was worn down. I could not make them learn times tables because they could not make themselves learn times tables. They had heard the voices of their teachers and perhaps their parents for years telling them to learn times tables. They heard the times tables themselves recited by these voices. But they did not internalize these voices.

On the one hand, they were told they should learn them. Failing to learn them must have brought on unpleasantness. On the other hand, they had the ability to learn them, perhaps not as fast as some of their peers, but the ability. That complex structure that Vygotsky posits was not developed in them, at least not the will to learn times tables. Perhaps they were listening to other voices, perhaps there were constellations of factors that prevented the development of will. They did not believe what one of our respondents said: "You gotta just do it."

CONCLUSION

So at the risk of being considered a bedfellow of those who self-righteously put the onus of school achievement and the improvement of education on students and little or none on the schools, or the educational or social system, who absurdly declare that success comes only to those who pull themselves up by their own bootstraps, I have suggested a theory of will to explain how students account for academic success. However, it is a very specific theory of will and not a simple definition. More importantly, I believe it is a helpful theory for researchers and teachers; we can perhaps find ways to keep the will intact. Moreover, for the students, it is a theory that tells them they are responsible for their own educations. If success is to mean anything to them, they must believe they are responsible for it.

Bruner (1987) does not believe that Vygotsky makes a convincing case for the centrality of language in the development of will. Luria (1987) sees Vygotsky's theory of will as "tentative." I suggested that student choice must go hand in hand with the voices they hear. But if Vygotsky's theory is not a popular one, if it does not answer all the questions about the motivation to achieve, it is, at least, as far as possible, an analog of the theory of our respondents who are operating on their "pretheoretical level[s] of consciousness" (Berger and Luckmann, 1967, p. 65). Vygotsky gives some justification for an emic theory of school success. Chapter 10 will give us an etic theory.

10

Voices, Selves, and Symbolic Universes

The stated purpose of this book is to present a picture of the lives of young people in an inner-city environment who are experiencing some degree of academic success. But further, I try to explain that success and, in particular, describe what is *in* the young people themselves that accounts for it. In the last chapter, I presented how *they* themselves explained their relative success and framed their theory of will with that of Vygotsky. Since these young people are functioning cognitively on what Peter Berger and Thomas Luckmann (1967) refer to as a *"pre*theoretical" (emphasis added) level of consciousness regarding success and since Vygotsky's lecture on will is considered by some as introductory and tentative, I find it appropriate to present additional theory. What I hope to do in this chapter is to synthesize an etic theory that helps explain the academic success of the young people in this book and which may point to the kind of education which would enhance this success.

In the Introduction of this book I said I wanted to present and analyze my data under the rubric of "cultural psychology," such as defined by Jerome Bruner (1990). What is remarkable about Bruner is that he manages to simultaneously be both an eloquent elder statesman and a Young Turk of psychology. After retiring from Harvard, Bruner has set out on an intellectual adventure that leaves those of us in academic psychology far behind as we struggle to keep up while trying to disguise our envy. In his book, *Acts of Meaning*, he suggests that the Cognitive Revolution, which sought to resurrect the concept of "mind" that had been purged from psychology by the once dominant behaviorists, had itself bogged down in computer models that reduce the mind to memory banks and processors located *within* the individual. It is significant, I think, that one of the positions Bruner has held since his "retirement" was the George Herbert Mead Professorship of Psychology at the New School for Social Research. For Mead (1922) objected to the mind being considered *within* and concluded that it "is. . .not confined to the individual. . .Significance belongs to things in their relations to individuals. It does not lie in mental processes which are enclosed within individuals" (p. 163). If Bruner and Mead are correct, we must redefine our question of what is *in* these young people that accounts for their success; "in," to the cultural psychologist more accurately means "in the interactions of."

Bruner (1990) argues for a cultural psychology that would be primarily concerned with "action situated in a cultural setting" rather than "behavior," especially that investigated in laboratories. One facet of this cultural psychology is "folk psychology" which can also be called "common sense." The folk psychology of any culture consists of normative descriptions that explain things like why people do what they do. The young people of this study trying to explain school success with the concept of will is an example of folk psychology. By invoking Vygotsky, perhaps the first cultural psychologist, I hoped to bring some theoretical rigor to these young people's explanations. I should state, incidentally, that one of the things that first led me to this seminal thinker was Bruner's enthusiastic introductions in several of the translations of Vygotsky's work.

AN ETIC VIEW OF SUCCESS

Certainly, an etic view of inner-city success must present, in addition to folk psychology, a multiple-frame theory to make it accessible and meaningful to the widest possible audience. For this I will use three frames: 1) symbolic universes as defined by Berger and Luckmann (1967) in their groundbreaking book, *The Social Construction of Reality*, in combination with mental representations of reality as defined by Gilles Fauconnier (1985) in *Mental Spaces*, 2) the self theory that organizes this study, and 3) the possibility of different young people hearing different voices, as suggested by Carol Gilligan (1982).

Symbolic Universes and Mental Spaces

Elsewhere (Farrell, 1990), I attempted to formulate a theoretical explanation of why some students, perhaps the majority in the inner city, fail to find success in school. In so doing, I used dialogue to present a picture of the cultural settings those young people found themselves in and I suggested they created different meaning systems in these settings than did successful students. The cultural settings in which the "folk" dialogues of this book take place are the same as those of the less successful students. But their actions in these settings are driven by systems of meanings that include access to more school in the form of higher education, future success, a greater variety of affiliations, and delayed gratification. These are actions based on legitimate beliefs. The at-risk students I studied, however, did not find these to be particularly meaningful to their lives. Although they often voiced the belief that there is a link between school and career, they did not act on it; their affiliations did not go much beyond their peers; few spoke to anything that could be described as delayed gratification.

Legitimation, as defined by Berger and Luckmann (1967), is the process, first found on a personal level, used to objectify social meaning. It establishes cognitive validity for the meanings we ascribe to our acitons. The establishment of "symbolic universes" is the highest level of legitimation. Symbolic universes are bodies of theoretical tradition that explain the realities that go beyond everyday experience. These "bodies of tradition" become overarching systems of meaning that allow for the understanding and the integration of biographical experience in terms of the world in which they live. On the level of folk psychology, the symbolic universe, to use the words of Berger and Luckmann, "puts everything in its right place" (p. 98).

Symbolic universes begin to be created in the family, are expanded in part in churches and other social agencies, and are codified in formal education. They can be elaborated on or undermined in peer interactions. But if social institutions are successful, the entire society should make sense to individuals at some point in their development. I suggest that this is very difficult for a minority student in the inner city. The more successful the young person is as a student, the more knowledgeable he will become. The more knowledgeable he is, the more he will realize that the meanings he has of school do not always make sense. That there are more African-American males aged twenty to twenty-nine in jail, on parole, or on probation than in college, that the unemployment rate for African-American males is more than twice that for whites (Goleman, 1992) must shake some of the meanings that the African-Americans among these young people attribute to education: school gives access to more education and career success.

Symbolic universes are handed down one generation to another and the universe that is handed down in school is largely that of the teachers. Berger and Luckmann (1967) realize, however, that some people "inhabit" the transmitted universe more definitely than others. When I compared at-risk to successful students in my previous study, using data gathered by and from the at-risk students, I suggested that successful young people were those who inhabited the transmitted universe more. This was, in fact, one of the explanations I offered to explain school success and failure. The successful students, I assumed, were not driven to construct what Berger and Luckmann consider an intrinsic problem in transmitting symbolic universes from one generation to the next: the creation of a deviant version of the universe that is shared by groups of inhabitants.

It would seem that the symbolic universe that the greater society is attempting to pass down to these young people is problematical. The symbolic universe of the United States of America assumes equal opportunity in the quest for life, liberty, and the pursuit of happiness. If a young person despairs of this, she will no longer be able to inhabit that symbolic universe; nothing will be in its right place. None of the voices of these young people—and few of the less successful students in my previous study, for that matter—seem to have despaired yet; the at-risk students were still, after all, in school. But our prisons are full of people who have despaired and the ever-present homeless beggars on the streets remind us that there is indeed reason to despair.

When there are such problems, say Berger and Luckmann, conceptual machineries of universe maintenance are produced in social activity by the collectivity, in this case the greater society through its schools, its social service institutions, and its communications media. Berger and Luckmann do not try to describe all the possible kinds of universe maintenance but they outline four types of this conceptual machinery that they consider conspicuous in all societies: mythology, theology, therapy, and nihilation.

Mythology.   The conceptual machinery of mythology acts on the most naive level of universe maintenance, according to Berger and Luckmann (1967). An example of such a myth can be found in *The Iliad* when Achilles did not kill Agamemnon, the king who had stolen his woman; the myth acted to maintain the political order of the Greeks. Myths of eternal rewards act to help people tolerate dreadful lives. In our culture, the Horatio Alger myth, even though unknown by that name by most of our respondents, is still with us. A poor boy can succeed if he remains pure of heart and works hard. Any boy (but not necessarily girl in this maxim) can grow up to be president. At-risk students might find this hard to believe and even the young people of this study need a caveat to make it palatable: "Not *everyone* can achieve success; only those of us who are deserving and who have the will."

Theology.   Theology is more sophisticated than mythology and usually has a historical base. As universe maintenance, it did little for the at-risk students of my previous study. The Protestant ethic that the most worthy will achieve material success is a myth on more naive levels but was actually codified by Puritan theologians. The young people in this study are too sophisticated to take Horatio Alger seriously but they may hear the same message from their clergy as well as their teachers. Even those churches that organize communities, even those that make up the basis for gaining political power, even the pastor-father of Carrie in chapter 4 who somehow gives the message that if you are hit, kill, even those contribute to the maintainance of the staus quo. They represent the establishment in the inner-city and, for very good reasons, they have more alliances with those in political power than antagonisms. The political reality is that confrontations, even antagonistic ones, are for leverage *within* the system.

The religions that most of these young people subscribe to have built-in caveats that enable members to maintain their symbolic universes in spite of glaring inequalities. Sharon, the first person interviewed in chapter 1, saw two kinds of people in the world, the bad and the good. "The bad is going nowhere. They're going straight to hell anyway, so I basically, I do that [succeed] so that when I get older I won't have to live in the situations I'm living in now." The Horatio Alger myth takes on a theology. And, of course, as a church member, Sharon is surrounded by "good" people. The saving grace of the conversion religions of many of these young people is that there is saving grace. Redemption and forgiveness are always and everywhere possible.

Therapy. If an individual has difficulty maintaining a symbolic universe, hers is a case for therapy. Therapy, in our culture, attempts to change the individual so that she can adjust to society. But in order for there to be therapy, there must be a theory of deviance. Psychoanalysis, for example, offers a theory of deviance for those who cannot or who choose not to maintain monogamous relationships. Adolescent pregnancy, a possible economic—but surely not a biological—problem in itself, has come to be considered a pathology by many educators and policymakers. The same thinking is often applied to the homeless. This allows us to see these phenomena as individual maladjustments rather than as social problems. Dropping out of school to work, once the norm for young people in America, is now considered deviant behavior.

Although Berger and Luckmann (1967) define therapy as universe maintenance for *individuals*, I suggest that there is also a kind of cultural group therapy operating in inner-city education. This therapy comes in the form of alternative schools, alternative programs within existing schools, magnet schools, schools for existing groups like African-American males. Some of these are for young people already considered deviant and some are preventive. The dropout prevention program from which I drew the student-collaborators for my at-risk study was both of these. As such, its task was very difficult; not many of its students had enough of a symbolic universe to maintain. Creating one for a seventeen-year-old ninth grader who had less than 10 percent of the credits needed for graduation was next to impossible.

I should point out that I do not consider the elite schools of New York, public or private, examples of this cultural group therapy even though they might be therapeutic for certain individuals. These may be excellent schools but, for the most part, they assume they do not have to contend with deviant universes. I suggest that their students deal with problems of inequalities for minorities by believing that our society is a meritocracy. They adopt the orientation that Fine (1991), cited in chapter 8, attributed to the successful students she called "graduates": they give themselves a privileged place by distinguishing "us" from "them" as do, of course, our respondents. In the final chapter of this book, I will describe schools that are examples of cultural group therapy.

Nihilation. One of the definitions of nihilation that Berger and Luckmann (1967) offer is negative legitimation. Legitimation maintains the reality of the symbolic universe; nihilation denies it. Those who doubt that success in school leads to future success are assigned an inferior status; the "us" and "them" dichotomy comes into use. This works best for people outside the inner city. They can believe that the inner city has a large immigrant and non-English-speaking population, a large black population, a large population of "others." However, this is more difficult when both "we" and "they" are members of the same minority group and often live in the same neighborhoods. In this case, what Berger and Luckmann refer to as a more ambitious type of nihilation becomes necessary: incorporation.

Incorporation is a type of conceptual machinery, in which the deviant representations of reality are accounted for in terms of the desired symbolic universe. School success *does* lead to career success except when the family breaks down, when babies have babies, when parents fail to read to their children, speak to their children, or hug them, all of which were the complaints of teachers interviewed in chapter 7. The deviant version of the universe is accounted for by concepts belonging to the approved version; the deviant version is thus annihilated by accounting for it, incorporating it into, and thereby affirming the official version of the symbolic universe.

Mental Representations of Reality

Berger and Luckmann (1967), in their desire to dispense with semantic intricacies, define reality simply as that which exists independent of our own volition. A symbolic universe is a cognitive construction that gives meaning to reality. Universe maintenance is a socially constructed conceptual machinery for creating meaning. Berger and Luckmann, however, do not tell us specifically—nor do they claim to do so—just how these meanings and concepts are constructed. But since these meanings and concepts are social, we can assume they are constructed in and by social interactions, both linguistically and often in many other subtle ways.

Fauconnier (1985), in *Mental Spaces*, defines reality itself as a mental representation but offers no equivalent to symbolic universes. However, he presents a very detailed theory on how mental representations are constructed. For this, he introduced the notion of *mental spaces* which are built up according to guidelines established by linguistic expressions but are distinct from linguistic structures. A symbolic universe, I suggest, consists of connected mental spaces. How the connectors work is persuasively and carefully explained in his book. His work led George Lakoff (1985) to say that Fauconnier's *mental spaces* succeed in explaining meaning where world semantics and situation semantics do not. This concept is not the subject of my investigation but what is important is the role of language in the development of mental spaces and, by extension I suggest, in the development and maintenance of symbolic universes. "Linguistic expressions," Fauconnier says, ". . .establish new spaces, the elements within them, and the relations between the elements" (p. 17). What students read but primarily, I think, what is *said* to them is what makes up symbolic universes.

I further suggest that teachers have one symbolic universe, meaning system, or group of connected mental spaces of longtime standing; successful students have another; less successful students have yet another. The three groups share the common physical space of the high school in which there are three mental spaces which overlap to some degree. The teachers and the successful students, I would argue, have the biggest overlap of the three; the successful and the less successful students have the next biggest; the teachers and the less successful students have the smallest. It is in the overlaps, of course, that we teach. The symbolic universes have been built up over the years and are maintained in daily discourse and in the teaching-learning experience. It would be as difficult to expect dramatic changes in them in short periods of time as it would be to hear dramatic changes in language patterns in similar short periods. Moreover, each group has constant peer support in the form of folk psychology to maintain its symbolic universe.

The Integration of Selves

The self theory I synthesize to structure this book can easily be integrated into the theories of Berger and Luckmann. Because the antecedents for it are largely drawn from psychology (Gergen, 1967, 1972, Markus and Nurius, 1986; Sullivan, 1953), I use the word "self" to denote the phenomena I am describing. If my parent discipline were sociology, I might use the word "role" instead of "self." Berger and Luckmann acknowledge their debt to Mead (1934) when they discuss "role" which they define as "typifications of performances." Mead seemed to use the word "self" both to distinguish it from "other" and as a totality as well, much like I am using the word "identity." It is, of course, well known that Erikson (1963), who gave us the term ego identity, uses the term "role confusion" as the negative side of identity formation in adolescence. And it is role confusion that hinders further development.

Hazel Markus and Paula Nurius (1986), drawing partially from Kenneth Gergen's (1967, 1971) notion of a changing self-image, posited a "now" self and a number of "possible selves." Possible selves can be positive or negative: the creative self, the rich self, the thin self versus the incompetent self, the alcoholic self, the bag-lady self. "Development can be seen," they suggest, "as a process of acquiring and achieving or resisting certain possible selves" (p. 955). Possible selves are people's ideas of what they might become, would like to become, or are afraid of becoming. The possible self, they further suggest, may provide a conceptual link between cognition and motivation. To argue that there is a single self that can be realized by an individual, according to Markus and Nurius, "is to deny the rich network of potential that surrounds individuals" (p. 965).

My possible pediatrician self might motivate me to do well in high school so that I can go to college and then medical school. We have heard two graphic descriptions of negative possible selves in chapter 1 which, it would seem, could motivate young people to do well. One description was given by a successful student and the other by an at-risk student from my previous study. Each invoked the specter of a homeless beggar, what Sullivan (1953) would have called the terrifying *not-me*, the concept that was introduced in chapter 1. But if both students have the same nightmare, why does only one of them act on his negative personification and apply himself to school more?

The answer, I think, is that a negative possible self, as terrifying as it may be, does not supply enough motivation; there must also be positive selves that can be integrated into a whole. By way of summary, I would like to compare the two groups in terms of the six selves identified in this study: sexual, peer, career, family, student, and affiliating.

The Sexual Self.   Both groups of students have sexual selves; those in this study speak more of boyfriends and girlfriends or of delaying their gratification. The boys in the previous study seemed to want to assure their interviewers that they were sexually active; the girls were less committal. But delayed gratification does not mean a person has less of a sexual self; he still has the raging hormones of adolescence and the intrusive fantasies. Not many young people in either group seem to have yet fully integrated their sexual selves into their identities. This lack of integration is what we would expect of adolescents in our culture; we do not, perhaps for good reason, make it easy for adolescents to have full sexual lives.

The Peer Self.   In the study of at-risk students, the peer self seemed to be presented in interviews with more intensity than any other self. The loyalty and caring that some of those young people demonstrated toward friends was admirable and, even in some cases, noble. That is not to say this behavior was lacking among the successful students. Kara's interviewer in chapter 3 cared enough about her to be willing to risk losing her friendship and stated she would tell Kara's parents if she thought her friend were making harmful life-style decisions. Apparently, she had integrated her family and her peer self. But the successful students were also realistic about peers and knew they had to sometimes choose their friends with discrimination.

Career, Family, and Student Selves.   The more successful students seemed better able to integrate these three selves. For them, a student self led to a career self; school success and career choice were supported by their families. Few of the at-risk students spoke of a future career but few adults knowledgeable about careers have probably spoken to them about such choices. The load of guidance counselors is too large for them to do much beyond academic counseling; career guidance is not often addressed in many high schools (Lee and Eckstrom, 1987; Powell, Farrar, and Cohen, 1985). Many less successful students reported family friction but this does not necessarily mean they did not have fully developed family selves. A number of the successful students, as well, reported family problems. Young people who do not have a history of success in school can hardly be expected to have developed a career self. If you fail your biology course, your teacher will not encourage you to become a doctor and, if you fail other courses, you may not develop much of a student self.

A possible self exists in a mental space which, according to Fauconnier, can only be created linguistically. Someone must talk to you about your possibilities. Bruner (1990) tells us that a self can only be revealed and realized in a transaction between teller and told. You construct and integrate your various selves socially. If I, because of inability or lack of exposure, read very little, if the only people I have extended conversations with are my friends, who know about as much as I do of the world, I will have a difficult time going beyond my peer group in my quest for an identity.

The Affiliating Self. Young people from each group can make strong affiliations. The successful student appears to make a greater variety of affiliations and may be more willing to let go of them. These are the young people who are expected to leave old friends, acquaintances, and associations and make new ones in college. The young people in this study tend to affiliate more with adult-oriented groups which help maintain their symbolic universes. The less successful student tends to affiliate with his immediate friendship group, the group he "hangs out" with. But he too loses friends as they drop out of school, become parents, go to jail.

By the time the successful student graduates from high school she has forged an identity, even if a tentative one. She may change colleges, change career orientations, or have a baby, but she is still a potentially good student, still a member of a family, still an aspiring professional. The less successful student may not have been able to do this and the tragedy here is that he has a greater and more immediate need to form an identity. For the successful student, college is a moratorium; she does not have to get a job immediately. The less successful student looks for a job he has not been able to define in an economy that is not very welcoming.

How many selves do I need to develop to have a sustaining identity? What selves have to be integrated in order for a young person to develop into an adult? I suggest that for young people in the inner city, the development and integration of the student and the career selves is essential; education must be linked to the prospect of a career. And this has to be a conscious cognitive link. This link is what Markus and Nurius (1986) believe makes motivation (read, will) possible. But making the cognitive link is not enough. What enables these young people to act is what they are calling will. A family that provides the basic necessities and supports young people's decisions offers an environment that might make the development of will possible. A community, whether it be school or church based, whether it be a group of friends, whether it be an after-school center, can support or replace a family and provide input for the cognitive linkage and give meaning to the decisions a young person makes.

It may seem like a platitude to say that young people need to see the connection between school and career. But, in fact, the majority of inner-city youth either apparently fail to make this connection or do not have enough support and reinforcement to act on it. Few people can make the cognitive link alone and fewer can act on it without support. After a young person's material needs have been met, she must be able to hear enough voices so that she can pick out the meaningful and "right" ones. The right voices, however, in the exigencies of inner-city life might well be the more muted ones. The young person might have to listen for *other* voices.

The Different Voice

Not all the elements of the different voice described by Gilligan (1982) fit the voice that the young people of this study seem to be heeding. But that is to be expected, I think. Gilligan's conclusions are largely based on her study of young women contemplating having abortions and she cautions that her data were gathered at a particular moment in history; her sample, she reports, was small (29 people); it was not randomly selected. As such, she is not willing to generalize. But her concept of different people, whether they be men or women as in her investigations, whether they be rich or poor, whether they be academically successful or not, hearing different voices and discerning different ways of making moral decisions, different modes of relating self to other, gives us another possible way of differentiating between two groups.

Gilligan's different voice spoke to creating social networks as opposed to a voice that speaks to relationships being easily replaced; it spoke to judgments being made on the basis of empathy rather than on logic; it spoke to a morality based on caring for others. This is not quite the voice that the young people in this study are heeding. Using Gilligan to describe the young people in this study as making a transition from selfishness of childhood to the responsibility of adulthood, as we did in chapter 3, is perhaps another way to differentiate between the groups but we have no evidence, except by inference, that at-risk students are *ir*responsible. They may be very responsible or potentially responsive to some voice, perhaps a voice they have not yet heard.

Gilligan suggests that men and women may, in the moral sense, speak different languages and because these languages share an overlapping moral vocabulary "they contain a propensity for systematic mistranslation" (p. 173). Women's lives, she thinks, have a different reality or what I refer to as different but overlapping mental spaces which translate ultimately to symbolic universes. Is the difference between the two groups we call men and women greater than the difference between the groups we call successful and failing students in inner-city schools? Not necessarily, I think. The voices I heard in my last study suggested a very different mode of thinking than do the voices I hear from these young people. I can only assume they are listening to different voices.

Gilligan defines the essence of moral decision—and I would say any decision about how to live one's life—as the exercise of choice and the willingness to accept the responsibility for one's choice. In making such decisions both groups must hear the different voices. But I suggest that the young people of this study heed the different voice because they actually have more choice than their less successful peers. Although I tried to negate the argument that they have more intelligence when I questioned the existence of such a phenomenon in chapter 9, I think it is obvious, as I pointed out in chapter 6, that they have acquired more tool use, which in this case means more academic skills. If you read at four hundred words per minute with ease and fluency, you have more choice in whether you will finish your assignment than your counterpart who stumbles along at one third your speed.

Like Gilligan, I will caution about trying to universalize these conclusions. My data, like hers, were gathered at a particular moment in these young people's lives as they try to survive in an inner city with a declining economic base. But Chicago, Los Angeles, and other cities may not be like New York. Some cities have huge adolescent populations that have recently arrived from other cultures and they might hear still other voices. In other cities, young people might have to deal with pressures to become members of large criminal street gangs which, at least, does not seem to be a problem for either of the groups of young people I investigated. There are obviously many different voices; the one I refer to represents a general mode of social interaction, of thinking, of decision making which can grow distinct enough in the course of adolescent development to be an analyzable factor on its own in accounting for success and failure.

Just as Gilligan's different voice can be interpreted by some as feminine and, thereby, devalued, can the voice these students heed be devalued by their less successful peers? The answer to this is yes; it is the voice for nerds; it is the voice of those who can, on some level, be seen as oppressors; it is the voice of conformity; it is the voice of a different generation—of pastors, teachers, mothers, and all those people who are believed to know little about life on the streets. And perhaps, it is a feminine voice as well. To heed it might mean, to young men, giving up hard-won stature in one group and seek it in another which, by adolescence, might not be very welcoming.

THE CULTURAL PSYCHOLOGY OF VOICE, SELF, AND SYMBOLIC UNIVERSES

Bruner (1986) believes that what he calls cultural psychology can shed light on the nature of the self. The self, he suggests, did not exist before philosophers and psychologists tried to describe it; it is not an observable entity. To the cultural psychologist, the self is a transactional relationship between one individual and another and is, therefore, dialogue dependent. The various selves of the young people whose voices we hear are created in dialogue by the voices themselves. A self, Bruner goes on to say, comes to be located both in private consciousness and in the cultural-historical situation. It is constructed from culture to mind as well as from mind to culture but always in action (or experience) which is continuous with a cultural world.

The voices that we heard have been incorporated into and come out of the self-systems of these young people. The integration of selves (e.g., the young person who is integrating a career and student self says, I am a student who will go on to college and become a pediatrician; if I am successful here, I will be successful there) is accomplished by, and further constructed into, a symbolic universe. Without hearing the appropriate voices and without, from such voices, being able to learn of, to adopt, and to adapt a symbolic universe, an individual may not be able to integrate her various selves into an identity.

A young person who puts all of himself (his selves) into peer relationships (or into his family or his girlfriend, for that matter) can find only a limited identity. This is what Rosie complained of when she found herself being referred to as "Bill's girl" by many of her peers. The symbolic universe for Bill's girl or for a mamma's boy is likely to be opaque and cannot be relied upon to "put everything in its place." More than one self must be integrated in order to begin to realize the symbolic universe. Relying on only one self may lead to the creation of a deviant universe, especially if coconstructed only with other single-selved people.

The symbolic universe, of course, has a prior existence. But young people must be able to see a logic and a goodness to what is handed down to them. Because of the many glaring inequalities, violence, and badness that young people in the inner city experience every day, many of them cannot accept the universe that is handed down. I suggest that the successful student must engage in what Harry Stack Sullivan (1953) referred to as "selective inattention" in order not to be confused or depressed by the often illogical, hypocritical, and sometimes evil universe that they hear from voices of other generations, other races, other social classes.

The inability to engage in selective inattention might explain why there are comparatively so few successful students in the regular zone high schools in the inner city. Can we then have schools where students hear a variety of voices, where they have choice and real autonomy to develop what they think of as "will," where they can coconstruct "possible" selves in a "possible" symbolic universe, where they can integrate their various selves into an identity as far as their age and experience will permit? A possible answer to this question will be found in the next chapter.

11
Small Is Better

The question that was asked at the end of the last chapter was, how can we have schools that work? A "how" question like this generates even more questions. Can we use what we have learned from the voices of the inner-city students in this book to create schools where higher percentages of young people succeed? Can we find good schools to serve as functioning models to improve others? The answer to both these questions is yes but a "how" question also generates dichotomous questions which require making choices. Can we build on what has succeeded in the inner city or do we have to start from scratch? Do we have to create totally new schools or can we transform already existing ones?

The answer to the latter questions is also yes. Some schools must be started from scratch. The two schools I will describe in this chapter were. But we cannot expect to replace every one of our existing schools with a new one; we do not have the resources. We may have to create some number of new schools but we can also use some already existing ones as models of reform. Ultimately, however, we will have to transform most of the urban schools that we have and most of the teachers that we have into something else. For the moment, I will call this "something else" a collection of communities of learning where young people will learn to use the tools of their technology and participate in what John Dewey (1897) called "the social consciousness of the race" (p. 77).

NEEDS OF STUDENTS AND TEACHERS

The community for learning should be an environment which aids the young person in integrating his various selves. It must be a democratic community where student voices are listened to, where the voices of knowledgeable and autonomous adults of integrity are heard and young people have choices in what they learn, where students and teachers together become aware of "the social consciousness of the race" and together construct a symbolic universe which has meaning for everyone in the community.

The Integration of Selves

To integrate one's often competing selves into an identity is a difficult thing to do in a crowd. In chapter 6, a number of students referred to this.

Ginny: I don't think they're giving the education that they should because they're too big. . . .
Perry: Everything's too big and rushed.
Vanessa: Cause everything's crowded, you know, impersonal.

Assuming we had smaller schools or small self-contained units within larger schools, how can we create an environment that is conducive to self-development and self-integration? Obviously, school should take into account what we know about "self" in young people.

Since the school-career link seems to be such an important motivating factor and the development of a career self so crucial to the formation of an adolescent's identity, high schools should build on it. For the 50 percent of the students in the United States who do not go to college, I would like to see more direct school-career links in the form of vocational education that prepares young people for real jobs. But of course, the half that the respondents of this book are drawn from needs to see the more complex link of school-higher education-career. In doing this, we should avoid negative incentives, for example, study hard so you won't become a street beggar. I have suggested that the *not-me* of Harry Stack Sullivan that was described in chapter 1 is too anxiety producing to act as an incentive. Positive rather than negative reinforcement, then, and access to career information are essential to self-development. It would seem that this should go without saying but, in fact, at-risk students in my previous study (Farrell, 1990) seemed to have no access to career information.

Development of the sexual self must take place in school as well as out. Although we did not encounter any pregnancies in our dialogues, about 40 percent of the adolescent girls who drop out of school cite pregnancy or motherhood as the cause (Pittman, 1988). AIDS makes sex education mandatory. But there is more that a school can do than sex education classes. An attitude must be presented that recognizes sexual behavior as part of human existence. It is all right to be a virgin or not to be one. To date or not. It is all right for a person to be homosexual. The major lesson in any version of sex education is what should be the major lesson of school—one must take responsibility for one's decisions and actions.

Since the peer self can become dominant in many young people, schools should endeavor to be social centers in their students' lives. The old-fashioned school dance is largely a thing of the past in urban areas. What teacher wants to come into the inner city at night to a social event that is likely to draw armed young people under the influence of various substances? But a small school can develop a rich and varied social program that can act as a bonding force among students and teachers. In addition, regular group advisement, conducted by teachers in familylike situations, can prevent young people from being pulled between the cracks by social and educational problems that would otherwise not come to anyone else's attention.

The family must be drawn into the school. Parents must come to believe that their children's school is special because their children are special. Parents must visit the school if they want their children to attend even on the high school level. To be sure, there are special cases where this is impossible but in a small school such cases can be identified and remedial action taken. Since virtually all parents want the best for their children, it must be made known to them what the demands of school are so they can support those demands. Cases where there are parent-child problems can be more easily identified in a small school and referrals made for mediation and/or therapy.

A student self that will follow the individual throughout life can only be developed where the individual has autonomy over that which she learns. Paul Goodman (1968) once declared that "nothing can be efficiently learned, or indeed, learned at all. . .unless it meets need, desire, curiosity, or fantasy" (p. 73). The curriculum of too many urban schools is test-driven; the day-to-day goal is that of social control. Contrast this to John Dewey's (1963) conclusion that "control of individual actions is effected by the whole situation in which individuals are involved, in which they share and of which they are cooperative or interacting parts" (p. 53). To use one of Dewey's metaphors, young people play by the rules when the rules are part of the game; when the game would disappear if the rules disappeared.

In the game of knowledge, the rules are determined by what the individual needs. When I chose to do my doctoral study on motivation, I needed to learn multiple regression to prove my points. The rules called for it. But if the rules are outside the game and arbitrarily imposed—if I were assigned to a course on regression, if I had to come to class, sit in an assigned seat, take off my hat, and complete successive work sheets on variables, coordinates, and equations that were not linked to my research—the learning process would have become boring to me and much time would have been wasted. Teachers should be resources for the development of student selves, not rule imposers.

In an interactive environment, the self that reaches out and makes affiliations will develop spontaneously along with career, sexual, peer, family, and student selves. Young people's voices must be listened to if we expect them to listen to the voices of others. If we want them to make affiliations there must be like-minded people for them to affiliate with. In school there are other young people and teachers. But this cannot be the complete universe for our students. School must reach out to the community and students must experience the community within their learning contexts and eventually meld them together. The school and the surrounding community together must become the community for learning that was introduced above.

Democracy, Autonomy, and Choice in the Comprehensive School

Democracy, autonomy, and choice are but platitudes in large urban schools operating in deplorable conditions. The words of Ginny, Perry, and Vanessa bear repeating therefore.

Ginny: I don't think they're giving the education that they should because they're too big. . .
Perry: Everything's too big and rushed.
Vanessa: Cause everything's crowded, you know, impersonal.

In light of these comments, I suggest that only in smaller schools can the three terms, democracy, autonomy, and choice, that start this section be realized.

The large comprehensive high school was developed for the best of reasons. The larger the school, the more teachers; the more teachers, the greater variety of course offerings; the greater the variety of course offerings, the more choice students have. It was thought that there would be much less duplication of effort if schools were consolidated. The consolidated tax dollars could buy advanced equipment that would be too expensive for small schools. There would be more social and extracurricular activities. There would be a large sports program to build a sense of community. There would be a critical mass of individuals for a student government that would mirror the political system. And indeed, there are some wonderful large comprehensive high schools that offer a superior education.

But large inner-city schools with diminishing resources are often counter-productive to insuring a good education. The bigger the school—especially a large school with a reduced staff—the more likely it is that students will fall between the cracks. Students in such schools sometimes seem to get fewer choices; Natalia in chapter 6 could not get into a Spanish class, probably the most commonly taught and certainly the most commonly spoken foreign language in New York. Extracurricular activities are the first things to go when budgets are cut. Democracy is a joke in a school where students have to be searched for weapons. For many students, the only autonomy they have is deciding whether to cut class or not or, ultimately, whether to drop out or not. It might be that the day of the large comprehensive high school, at least in urban areas, is over.

If the student explanation for school success is correct, young people must develop will. But will cannot be developed unless it is exercized and this occurs when young people have real choices. If they need to hear and internalize a variety of voices to develop will, as Vygotsky suggests, they will be less likely to internalize these in a crowded school where teachers act primarily as dispensers of information to passive vessels and everything is "rushed," to use Perry's word. Will and autonomy, I suggest, are synonomous. The young people in this book who talk about success vis-à-vis will might be the exceptions. Young people not granted autonomy in school have, by definition, no will as long as they remain there.

All students I have taught, even the very young, believed in taking a vote to decide certain classroom issues. The seeds of democracy are there. But none of the students in this book get to vote on any real issue outside of the classroom.

None of them get to vote on school rules and policy. Is it any wonder that so few people vote as citizens? Many of the at-risk students in my previous study believed in taking votes but they did not seem to have a general faith in democracy. If education is to prepare people to live in a democratic society, it has failed in many cases. And it has failed more conspicuously in the inner city. Obviously, the communities of learning that we need to create must be democratically based; young people must believe they have a voice and must be able to vote on issues that have real consequences.

The School-Society Universe

From my phenomenological point of view, symbolic universes are built from individual selves outward. But a symbolic universe is a historical phenomenon as well. What is built up in the family, among peers, and in the school must link up with and become part of the symbolic universe that makes life meaningful to the majority of people in the culture. The individual must participate in the cultural group consciousness. A social studies teacher might be able to describe the symbolic universe that, for him, gives meaning to the social world but it may be a rather abstract notion to many of his students. He may explain how society is democratic but his students are aware, on some level, that school is very often not.

I have no illusions that a large inner-city school can function on a democratic basis. And I am skeptical of A. S. Neill's (1960) claim that everyone at the Summerhill school, from himself to a three year old, had one vote on school issues and that such a vote had any real significance. But a small school has a better chance, I believe, to build a symbolic universe inhabited by all its students, that more closely reflects that of the greater society, and has a better chance of dealing with conflicts within and between symbolic universes. There is no way to build a symbolic universe that gives meaning or adequately explains the shooting deaths of two of your students at the hands of another in your school corridor.

When I suggested that we create communities of learning, I did not define "community." I now suggest a restricted definition of this word: a group where every member knows every other member. What Ginny, Perry, and Vanessa tell us is true. I do not believe that a symbolic universe that is meaningful to everyone can be created in a large school. The "learning" in these communities is the reason people—students, teachers, and parents—join them. I do not speak to the nature of the subject matter or the quality of instruction. That is not to say that these things are unimportant; need and interest should determine subject matter; a good teacher can teach anything. . .provided she is willing to learn it first. Develop the communities and the good teachers who are in the school system will flock to them. But to change the entire system, as I suggested above, we may have to train a new type of teacher.

RIVER EAST ELEMENTARY SCHOOL

Some years ago I founded and directed an alternative high school. I have written about this elsewhere and, suffice to say, I do not think we were successful. There were a number of reasons why this was so, including a foolish philosophy we had that freedom was the answer to everything in education. But it was equally foolish and presumptuous to believe that we could begin a new educational endeavor on the secondary level alone. Reform in education must start at the beginning of education; the brunt of our efforts must be in the elementary schools. In this section, I will describe a wonderful elementary school, one of only about two or three out of the six hundred or so schools in New York that I would send my own children to.

River East Elementary School, founded in 1982, is located in the East Harlem section of the city. The neighborhood was once Italian but is now mostly Latino; it can be described as poor and working class. River East is one of three unconnected schools, including a high and a junior high, in a large building that once housed a comprehensive high school. River East has a part of the second floor and a number of auxiliary rooms in other floors of the building. They have use of part of a cafeteria which also serves for school assemblies. The school is technically part of another elementary school in the district which, of course, has a principal, but it functions autonomously and independently with a director who is a teacher rather than an administrator. The staff refers to River East as a teacher collaborative.

River East has 230 students and 14 teachers. Classes are interaged so that a teacher can have the same student for two years. The configuration in 1991–92 was two pre-kindergarten-kindergarten classes, two first-second grades, one second-third, one third-fourth, one fourth-fifth, and two fifth-sixths. In addition to the classroom teachers, there is the director, an art teacher, a librarian/Spanish teacher, a special education teacher, and a computer teacher. The per-pupil expenditure is no greater than that of the citywide average.

Judicious budgeting allows River East to put a greater share of expenditures into teachers rather than administrators. Such budgeting also applies to books and materials. Rather than buying, say, twenty-five expensive hardcover textbooks for a class, River East is more likely to use the same amount of money or less to buy one hundred different paperbacks. The computer room has old computers, used computers, donated computers. The energetic faculty has generated grant funding for books and a renovation of the library, among other things. There is not much at River East that looks new; there is not much at River East that goes unused.

River East is both a district and a magnet school in New York. The New York City School system is divided into thirty-two geographical districts. As a district school, River East must take half its children from the district. As a magnet school it may draw from anywhere in the city. To gain admission to River East, the parent must apply. As part of this procedure, parents must visit the school where the academic program and philosophy are presented to them. The next step is for the parent and the child to visit the school. There are no psychological or academic requirements and the school has a cross section of children that reflects the racial, social class, and academic abilities of those of the city in general. As might be expected, there is now a waiting list for admission to most grades at River East.

It is true that the parents of the children at River East are informed enough about the New York City system to seek the school out. They have the energy and the desire to find what they think is the best possible placement for their children. It is also obviously true that the parents are highly supportive of the school. Even with the cross section of ability, it is probably true that family attitudes toward education go a long way toward insuring success in school. The teachers in chapter 7 and the parents in chapter 5 thought other parents were one of the greatest problems in education. River East, by and large, does not have to deal with that problem. But we do not expect a model school to confront every problem in education; we expect them to give us a model that will work in a number of other situations. There can be no one panacea for the myriad problems in urban education.

When one walks into River East, she sees activity everywhere. It is often not clear where the classrooms end and the corridors begin. Both classrooms and corridors are cluttered with computers, aquariums, children working on projects, easels, a sand table, animals in cages or on the floor, plants growing, books, blocks, vast and sundry articles, all the products or materials of children, all interesting. The walls are covered with charts, maps, and more children's products. In the spring semester of 1992, there was a self-portrait of every child in the school by class on the wall of the main corridor—a developmental psychologist's dream.

In classes, it is obvious that children's voices are valued. They are listened to and taken seriously. One of my City College students, a product of the New York City Public Schools, doing fieldwork at River East wrote in her log, "I immediately picked up how competent and confident the children were at expressing their feelings and ideas." Another of my students wrote, "I . . . found it surprising how the teachers knew most of the children even if they were not their students." Every Tuesday morning there is a whole school assembly at River East. It begins with a song; there are announcements and introductions; children are appraised of such things as city budgetary problems that may affect their school; anyone may speak. River East *is* a community for learning.

Within this community, teachers and students create classroom environments that are significantly supportive of children's active learning. The philosophy of River East seems to be based on a belief that the failures in our educational system come about because children do not find the often passive activities in schools meaningful to them. This is particularly true for cultural minorities—now the majority in New York—who have the added burden of making sense of an imposed culture with its competing mores, its mandated homogeniety, its implied judgments in the form of standardized tests, age norms, and ability grouping.

In much of their learning at River East, children conduct their own investigations directly on the phenomena to be studied. If a class is studying, say, the ecology of New York City, there may be a trip to see tidal pools and salt marshes. If a child becomes interested in the life of a salt marsh, he or she can create and have created one in an aquarium. The children have real choices in what they decide to study. This is not to say that basics are neglected. In my judgment, students at River East read and write more than in most other elementary schools I have seen. But reading and writing are means to an end, not ends in themselves. The students who created the salt marsh had to read about it; they had to find out how to set up a saltwater aquarium. It also seems to me that the students at River East are better trained at observing and recording their observations than other children I have seen in corresponding age groups.

What is happening at River East, I believe, is that the family, the student, and the peer selves of the children are developing in an integrated triad. As preadolescents, their career and sexual selves are rudimentary but they acquire knowledge of the world of work and the workings of gender, reproduction, and sexuality from their parents, their teachers, and their readings. They make affiliations among the members of their democratic community. They have more autonomy than children of most other schools and, as I said above, have real choices. They begin to construct, with their peers, teachers, and parents, a symbolic universe that makes what they do with their lives meaningful.

The graduates of River East go in a number of different directions. Some go to one of the elite schools in the city; some go to magnet junior high schools; some go to the regular junior high schools in the city that the parents think have good reputations; a few go to private schools. Many go to Central Park East Secondary School which is affiliated with River East through the Center for Collaborative Education in New York. The collaborative is composed of six elementary schools, each with a philosophy and practice much like that of River East, and nine secondary schools, including Central Park East Secondary.

CENTRAL PARK EAST SECONDARY SCHOOL

Central Park East Secondary School was founded by the nationally known educator, Deborah Meier. It consists of a junior and a senior high school. In practice, the school has three divisions: the seventh and eighth grades, the ninth and tenth grades, and the senior institute. As is the case at River East, students can stay with teachers for two years. Admission to the school is much like admission to River East. Its student body is representative of the demographic distribution of the city school system. The academic ability of its students is normally distributed. Like River East, it has a special education program; there are two resource rooms where students go for special help.

The school, like River East, is located in East Harlem. It shares a building with several other schools, including Central Park East I, an elementary school much like River East. The secondary school has approximately 450 students and 40 staff members. Staffing, however, is creatively designed. The number of administrative and support personnel is minimized and the number of direct-service teachers is maximized. By eliminating positions like that of assistant principal or guidance counselor which are more costly than teacher positions, a greater number of teachers can be hired. For example, a staff of 12 which includes an assistant principal, a guidance counselor, and 10 teachers, each with a class of 30, can be restructured as a staff of 13 teachers, each with a class of 23, for the same amount paid in salaries. In order for this to work, of course, the teachers must be willing to take the responsibility to carry out the former functions of the assistant principal and the guidance counselor.

Central Park East does not use the traditional departmental structure of most high schools and colleges. What would be English and social studies in a traditional school is humanities at Central Park East. Mathematics and science are grouped as well. This allows maximum flexibility and teacher collaboration in planning curriculum. Instead of individual teachers, working independently, each responsible to get some number of students through an assigned syllabus during an academic year, a team of teachers is responsible for the total education of a certain number of students. The team meets weekly to plan humanities and math-science units, to discuss student problems that arise in group counseling sessions, to oversee the education of the students it is responsible for. Each student has a faculty advisor who has no more fifteen students.

A humanities unit that was implemented in the spring of 1992 was a simulation of a fictitious Supreme Court case. Several groups of students argued the case from particular points of view. Another group presented counterarguments. A panel of students served as the justices. Each group was to collect facts and each student was to write an essay. Because humanities consists of two subjects which are scheduled-back-to back, the students had large blocks of time in which to work on the curriculum unit rather than a daily forty- or forty-five–minute period. Similar units have been made part of curricula in more traditional schools, of course, but the structure of Central Park East contributes to this type of creative teaching.

The curriculum at Central Park East is not test-driven; its students simply do not take the Regents examinations that were discussed in chapter 6. They do, however, take tests that measure academic skills and content. Apparently, this causes no great harm to them; even without a Regents diploma, every one of Central Park East's first graduating class was accepted into a college. The grading system is based on categories of effort labeled (D)istinguished, (S)atisfactory, and (U)nsatisfactory with pluses and minuses. But the graduation requirements for the Senior Institute is the completion of fourteen portfolio projects. These projects come out of their studies and are documents that might consist of papers, charts, maps, photographs, created objects. They represent an independent inquiry or experience of the student's choice. In addition, the student must present and defend seven of his projects before a committee of teachers.

According to the "Senior Institute Handbook" (1991) of Central Park East, the fourteen portfolio areas include the following: 1) Postgraduate Plan, 2) Autobiography, 3) School and Community Service and Internship, 4) Ethics and Social Issues, 5) Fine Arts/Aesthetics, 6) Practical Skills, 7) Media, 8) Geography, 9) Second Langauge, 10) Science/Technology, 11) Math, 12) History, 13) Literature, 14) Physical Challenge. Two examples of papers submitted in 1990 to fulfill the media and science/technology requirements were, respectively, "How Advertising and Consumerism Affect Individuals and Society Negatively" and "How Dust Mites Affect Asthma Victims."

It is essential in the Central Park East program that each student perform community service or experience an internship in area agencies or businesses. By doing so, students investigate career options. Community service has been performed in a school for the deaf, in a Kids-Meeting-Kids program at the United Nations, by working with a judge in the court system. Internships have been completed at TWA, Simon and Schuster publishers, Marvel Comics, Citibank. This, as stated above, becomes one of the portfolio areas. The symbolic universe that is created at Central Park East is part of the historical symbolic universe that gives meaning to the whole of society. The community for learning is not a closed community.

My City College students who attended traditional high schools react to Central Park East in a number of ways. A number of them carried out fieldwork in the school in the spring of 1992. One young man who had been educated in a Catholic high school was not impressed with the informality he experienced while observing the seventh-eighth grade. He wrote in his field notes, "I'd rather place my child in a school where I know that he is being taught discipline, respect, and manners." Another was concerned that the emphasis on individual responsibility did not benefit all students. Of one student, she wrote, "I began to think that John may be using the CPE way as a crutch for his laziness."

But most of my college students reacted very favorably. They were impressed with the level of books the students they observed read and the articulateness of the class discussions. But they saw something else within individual students that, as graduates of the city school system, they considered more important. One of my students described this in his field notes.

> Paul learned a lot about himself. He learned one must respect himself and others and must find out what one wants in life and live one's dream and don't let anyone take it away. He said it was important to be oneself and not try to be anyone but yourself.

Others reported very similar messages after they each had gotten to know one of the students.

Marla told me that Central Park East had built her self-esteem and motivated her to live her dreams. The school has made her aware of her own background and how important it is to know where one comes from. Marla can say with pride that she is a New Yorican [New York born Puerto Rican]. If she hasn't learned anything else, she has learned to love herself.

Central Park East might not be the answer for every student and it might not still be the answer for New York City students in five years. It may not be the answer for those who do not attend college. But if the school is nothing else, it is flexible. Its small size makes it more amenable to change. Like River East, it is constantly evolving. Because it has developed a sense of community, it attracts dedicated and creative teachers. There are none of the mediocre teachers there that Katie referred to in chapter 6 or burnt out cases reported by teachers in chapter 7. Dedicated and creative teachers in a flexible structure can reinvent education and they can keep reinventing it every five years or as often as is needed.

I do not suggest that every student at Central Park East successfully integrates all her various selves into an identity; I suggest that young people have a better chance of doing it there than in large urban schools. In a community of learners, the student self is central. But it is linked to a career self because of the emphasis on future education. With parent cooperation, the family self is, at least, not at odds with other selves. The students at Central Park East are surrounded by like-minded peers. They make affiliations with those peers, with teachers, with other people in the wider community. I am unable to speak to the integration of the sexual selves of these students. But if my student's description of Paul, above, is accurate and typical of the other students, the fact that he has learned to respect himself and others would bode well for the responsible development of this self.

RESTRUCTURING FOR SUCCESS

Critics of Central Park East point out that it is easier to start schools from scratch than to reform already existing schools. Deborah Meier (1992), the founder of Central Park East, responds to such criticisms by suggesting that they do the same thing as she and her teachers did; they should demand the same freedom in their schools that Central Park East has. River East, as I pointed out, is one of three separate schools in one building. What is to prevent a large high school of three thousand students from breaking up into ten small autonomous schools, all in the same building? Every four staff members could have total responsibility, including guidance, administration, and instruction, for, say, eighty students.

What would prevent this? Number one: educators and students unwilling to step out of the roles they have been constructed for and by them. Number two: fear of freedom and responsibility, neither of which can be given or taken without the other. Number three: the unwillingness to part with hard-won power, position, and sinecures. Number four: fear of failing. But Deborah Meier and her colleagues are neither giants, magicians, nor saints. I think that a large number of the teachers whose voices we heard in chapter 7 would be willing to cast off old roles, take the responsibility, and grasp the freedom they would need to make changes. If they fail, well, the system is failing now. It is hard to believe that such experiments would worsen the situation and action, I believe, is better than inaction.

But this book is about high school students. It is about young people who play by the rules of the game, imposed and otherwise, and achieve some degree of success. I applaud them for their success but I see no way that their numbers will increase under the present school structures. The will to succeed cannot create itself; it grows as the individual grows in an appropriate social setting. By and large, the inner city with all its social problems is not that setting nor are most inner-city schools. Although these young people have been able to integrate their various selves to one degree or another, those in my previous study could not. But perhaps their voices, even if they have not articulated a clear and complete vision of what education should be, can give us a starting point in a hazardous but necessary journey. Risking failure, we must begin to reform schools even as the final vision of what those schools should be is evolving. The way to change is an existential journey. And the great Spanish poet and mystic, St. John of the Cross, wrote on how to start such a journey.

> In order to get to a place that thou knowest not,
> Thou must go by a way that thou knowest not.

Appendix
Ethnographic Inquiry and Education

Ethnography is the creation of text to make some sense out of a culture. How the subject matter of the text should be chosen and investigated and what the text should look like are questions for which social scientists in the last decade of the twentieth century have no consensual answers. If there is any agreement on what constitutes an ethnography, it would be, I suppose, that the data for it be gathered by participant observation. Usually, it is the participant observer(s) who interpret(s) the data and prepare(s) the text. If this is not the case, the question arises as to the validity of the inquiry and, to a lesser extent, whether the resulting product can be called ethnography.

Although I was trained in the techniques of participant observation by Karen Watson-Gegeo, an anthropologist then at the Harvard Graduate School of Education, I was most interested in an interdisciplinary approach to inquiry in education and the social sciences. Because I have spent virtually all of my adult life as a teacher, I am primarily an educationist and I am attempting to adapt ethnography to inquire into issues of schooling. Moreover, my experience tells me that I am better able to do participant observation in some settings and among some populations than I am in others. My choices of setting and methodology, therefore, are not unlimited.

THE METHOD

Making Sense of a What?

It is not the purpose of this inquiry to define culture. In order to explain what we are doing here, let us simply take a dictionary type definition: the way of life of a society. But what society we are inquiring into in this study is problematic. Are we investigating adolescents? Inner-city adolescents? Inner-city adolescents of color? African-American adolescents? Latino adolescents? Immigrant adolescents? Or are we investigating a setting? Is the setting of one school enough like another so that we can say we are investigating urban schools?

Can any of these groups or settings qualify as being a culture or even a subculture?

Ethnography's root definition would have to be given as "writing about a people." The operant word of this definition is the indefinite article "a" which is absent in the root definition of demography; *ethnos* meaning a specific people and *demos* meaning people in general. I would argue that the term "inner-city adolescent" has been socially constructed by demographic investigators and the media. In complex societies like our own, ethnography must be informed by demography but the ethnographer attempts to find out if demographic contructions have an independent reality. Obviously, there are adolescents living in the inner cities of our country; most of them attend school; some of them are successful. The subjects of this inquiry, therefore, come from a statistically discrete population.

Whether they are a discrete subculture, however, is another question. In chapter 10, I used Berger and Luckmann's (1967) term "symbolic universe" where others might use "culture." I described the symbolic universes of teachers, of successful students, of "at-risk" students as overlapping. What we try to do in education and in the socialization process in general is increase the overlaps. So as I try to describe a discrete symbolic universe, I am also trying, as an educator, to lessen the discreteness. I want these young people to make sense of *our* common symbolic universe. In this respect, then, what I have done is not ethnography, per se. I believe, however, that my method of inquiry is valid.

Procedure

When I began my inquiry into inner-city public schools in 1986, I asked myself whether a white, middle-aged, middle-class academic could enter multiple settings made up of poor and working-class, African-American and Latino youth and gather sufficient intimate data on their lives to answer research questions like what makes students succeed, what makes them fail, how do significant others affect them. The questions I asked myself were for practical rather than political reasons and had to do with what I perceived as my personal strengths and limitations. Others may well be able to carry out participant observation in settings that would be difficult for me. In 1984–85, Michele Fine (1985, 1986, 1987, 1991) preceded me—although I did not know this when I started—in one of the schools in which I conducted my initial research. Her work, which was conducted by means of participant observation, has been both a model and an inspiration to me.

When I began looking systematically into urban education, I was attempting to gain some understanding that went beyond attendance records, test scores, promotion records, and guidance referrals, of a population drawn from a number of schools for which the City College was trying to set up an enrichment program. We needed to know something of the everyday lives of the population to be served in our program. Frederick Erickson (1986) proposes using an "interpretive" approach based on fieldwork when one is trying to find out what is going on in a particular place. He maintains that the interpretive approach asks different questions than standard approaches to educational research, such as the following:

> What are the conditions of meaning that students and teachers create together, as some students appear to learn and others don't. . . . How is it that it can make sense to students to learn in one situation and not in another? How are these meaning systems created and sustained in daily interaction? (p. 127)

But because I had reservations that I would be able to get valid answers to such questions and because of the practical consideration that I needed to gather data in a number of different places, preferably both in and out of school, I decided that I could not take the role of a traditional, participant-observing ethnographer. Traditionally, of course, ethgnographers have recruited actors from within the setting to act as informants and have gathered data from them. The use of informants offered a partial solution to my problem of relating to the students but did not deal with what I saw as a problem of data analysis done from a single subjective point of view. I needed collaborators who were intensely interested in the subject population, who could gather data in situations where I could not, and who could also be involved in the analysis of the data. In light of a question framed by Fine (1987), "What if the 'dropout problem' were studied in school as a collective critique by consumers of public education" (p. 171), I decided that my collaborators should be drawn from the subject population. Moreover, because of her conclusion that students were "silenced" when they dissented, I tried to give them a voice in the study.

From teachers and by word of mouth, I recruited student-collaborators from a dropout prevention program in one of the schools we were working with to engage in tape-recorded interviews with their peers. The interviews were anonymous and unstructured and were meant to be dialogues between individuals in the subject population rather than standard interviews. The dialogues were professionally transcribed. Collaborators were paid ten dollars an hour for their dialogues and for collaborating in the analysis of the transcribed data. The results of that study were summarized in a research article with my collaborators as coauthors (Farrell, Peguero, Lindsey, and White, 1988). A book followed that attempted to construct a theory on the causes of dropping out of school.

In constructing or adapting theory that answers questions like "What accounts for student success?" and "How do the lives of successful and unsuccessful students differ?" I would prefer to follow Barney Glaser and Anselm Strauss's (1967) dictum of having it arise from the data. This I did in my original study. The "theory" that came out of the at-risk study was the basis for the "self" paradigm that I outline in the Introduction and which became the framework for this book. But Patti Lather (1991) cautions that when building such "grounded" theory, while we are permitted the use of a priori theoretical frameworks, we must keep "a particular framework from becoming the container into which data must be poured" (p. 62). On the other hand, she states that because human actions are never fully rational and are often driven by unconscious forces, "[s]ole reliance on the participants' perceptions of their situation is misguided. . ." (p. 64).

From this we see that there might develop a tension between theory arising from data and existing theory when one attempts interpretive research. I try to resolve this by heeding Tyler's (1986) call for a "post-modern" ethnography in which the dialogue of participants is in the foreground, rather than the usual research monologue guided by "the ideology of the transcendental observer" (p. 126), usually a lone ethnographer. Tyler's type of ethnography results in a ". . .cooperatively evolved text consisting of fragments of discourse intended to evoke...a possible world of commonsense reality" (p. 125), referred to in the introduction of this book.

My theoretical framework, which Tyler might call "the ideology of the transcendental observer," is prominently stated. I would argue, however, that even if it were not, it would nevertheless be present. Were we studying fossils we would not bracket out Darwin and wait for a new theory to arise from the data. Even if we tried, Darwin would be there anyway as part of our "ideology." Neither can a study of adolescent development neglect all theorists in the field, especially if they impart meaning and continuity to the data.

The use of such "ideology" in teacher-student dialogues may be what C. A. Bowers (1984) calls "cultural invasion" (p. 96); the teacher (or adult researcher) simply has too much authority for there to be true reciprocity. It is what the three high school students and I (Farrell et al., 1988) tried to avoid by drawing interviewer-collaborators from the at-risk population to be studied. Robert Everhart (1977), in his study of junior high school students, suggests data-gathering techniques based on reciprocity between data gatherers and subjects to the point where they became friends. Ann Oakley (1981), interviewing women, maintains that there can be no intimacy at all without reciprocity; the interviewer is to share her own personal thoughts.

In order to gather data on the intimate lives of the "successful" students in the inquiry that informs this book, I followed my previous procedures and recruited collaborators from the population to be studied. Obviously, high school students could gather data from people and in places where I could not. In order to downplay the "ideology of the transcendental observer" and to reduce the tension between grounded theory and already existing theory, these collaborators were to be given little direct training in interview techniques and they were to decide whom to ask what in unstructured situations. They were to engage in reciprocal dialogues in which their utterances would also be analyzed as data. Moreover, as collaborators, they were to operate independently and not under direct supervision.

During the 1990–91 academic year, three practicing teachers in a graduate research course I teach volunteered to be research assistants in this study. They recruited five African-American and Latino, male and female high school students to act as interviewers. These students were identified by the teacher assistants as average and better students who were involved with school, were cooperative, had positive attitudes, and who wanted to attend college. The teachers approached them and asked if they would be willing to take part in the project for which they would be paid.

In my study of potential dropouts, I started out with both young men and young women but, because of attrition, ended with three male collaborators who were part of the same dropout prevention program. This was a limitation of that study which could not be helped. Here, four young women from three different high schools participated for the duration of the study and took part in the reduction of data as well. However, some of the interviews were collected by a young man who, because of other commitments, left the project. The reader will have to decide whether the "at-risk" study had a markedly masculine cast and whether this one has a markedly feminine cast because of who the collaborators were. I prefer to think that the "worlds" created in each book are "possible" and reflect the realities of the young people, both men and women, in them.

In this study, each student was given an audiotape recorder in order to interview, after assuring them anonymity, other high school students who were considered *by the interviewer* to be successful in school. They defined this simply as a student who was passing all his or her subjects and who, in the opinion of both interviewer and interviewee, was likely to graduate. The students were not in programs classified as "gifted" nor did they attend any of New York's elite high schools, although a few were in alternative programs within the public school system. Interviewers developed their own informal protocols for approaching other students. Below are two typical protocols.

> 1. Okay, basically I'm going to ask you questions about yourself, your home, school, church, everything. What else? If you have any questions just throw back a question. Anything I ask you, be descriptive and everything.
> 2. I'm helping a teacher out doing like a survey on why certain kids, certain underprivileged kids do better than other kids, but they're in the same situation, right? And you do pretty well in school and you don't have too much money, right?

Sixty-two dialogues were generated among sixty-seven students (counting interviewers) from seven high schools in three of the city's boroughs. Students were mostly African-American and Latino but there were two whites as well. Sixty-seven people are not a representative sample in a school system of one million but the previous study was based on a total of seventy-three. The study of teachers of the at-risk that was the basis for chapter 7 used sixty-four respondents and the one on the parents of at-risk students that is the basis for chapter 9 used sixty-three. Daphne Patai (1988) interviewed sixty Brazilian women of different ages, races, and social classes to learn from them "how their lives appeared to them" (p. 143). In light of this previous research, I suggest that the numbers are sufficient to evoke Tyler's "possible world of commonsense reality." Moreover, such numbers yield a manageable amount of data. All dialogues were professionally transcribed and there were some eight hundred pages of interview data to work with in addition to a similar amount of transcribed data from each of the studies (teacher and parent) mentioned above.

In the central (student) study, each of the four interviewers was given her own copy of all the transcripts. Each was asked to underline on that copy what were the most telling comments about a young person's life, including school, friends, parents, the future, or whatever else she thought was important. The four also indicated which of the comments they did not believe to be true. Following the methodology of my previous study, *data underlined by all four interviewers were considered the most crucial and analysis focused on these.* I believe this gives participants a greater voice in determining how their lives should be presented. Moreover, this method offers a triangulation of data on a master copy from which to isolate research categories. The underlined data were then coded and sorted into the appropriate categories, in this case, the defined selves.

Coding of data was done by hand on the master copy with colored pencils. At first the "self" categories of the at-risk study were used: career, sex, peers, family, student, and parent. Since no one in the data of this study was pregnant or a parent, this category was eliminated. In the course of reading and rereading the transcripts, however, two additional categories emerged: the one, "affiliations"—but which I now wish I had called by Carol Goodenow's (1992) term, "belonging" (hence, "The Belonging Self")—and the other, of course, "will." These were then coded. It was, of course, possible for the same data to serve in more than one category. This coding system was used, with different collaborators and categories, on the data gathered by teachers that inform chapter 7 and the data gathered by parents that inform chapter 5. The teacher-collected dialogue, however, was transcribed by the four teacher-collaborators who did the interviewing themselves. The underlined, coded segments were then blocked into potential chapters.

It should be noted that transcribing large amounts of data is expensive and labor-intensive. Because much of the interviewing was done in less-than-ideal conditions: noisy cafeterias, crowded halls, streets, even a professional word processor must replay the tapes numerous times. The teachers who did their own transcribing and who were obviously not professionals averaged eleven hours listening and typing to fully transcribe every hour of played-back tape. The work is tedious and exacting; the pay is never sufficient. But it is these technicians that fix discourse into text and the act of transcribing—even if done automatically—transforms the data from one medium with its own methods of (spontaneous) analysis to another with different methods of (reflective) analysis. Transcription is perhaps the most important single act in this type of inquiry.

THE TEXT

The Possible World

Ethnographic text often takes on a life of its own based on—but independent of—the data that inform it. To Paul Ricoeur, "...a text is detached from its author...and develops consequences of its own" (1981, p. 206). In this inquiry, the data are Tyler's "fragments of discourse." But once discourse is textualized, says James Clifford, "Interpretation [of, in this case, our fragments] ...does not depend on being in the presence of a speaker" (1988, p. 39). This brings us back to the question asked at the end of the first paragraph of this appendix as to whether this inquiry is valid and is an ethnography.

Although this study was collaborative in collecting and reducing data, there was only one drafter of the final text. I did not do the participant observation, for reasons stated above, but I did the interpretation and wrote the book. Depending on how seriously one takes Tyler, this book may be considered an ethography but I, the drafter, do not think that I am an ethnographer here. As I stated above, I am not not an anthropologist but an educationist practicing, in this case, interpretive cultural psychology as a means of preparing a book that contributes to the understanding of the phenomenon of school success in the inner city.

Does the book represent a "possible world?" This may be another way of asking whether the research is valid. I believe that the use of student-collaborators enables us to answer this question in the affirmative. However, one must ask if there is anything "impossible" in it. Again, many "impossibilities" were eliminated by my collaborators in their reduction of the data. The material and conclusions do not seem to conflict with previous research, with the combined experience of my three research assistants who are teachers, or with my own, albeit subjective memories.

Since we addressed the question of validity, we should also address that of reliability. Would other collaborators collect different fragments of discourse? Of course. But would those fragments offer an alternative "possible" world? The triangulation achieved by having each collaborator independently underline what she considered the crucial aspects of the data and the fact that the data were gathered in seven different schools speaks to this. Another factor which, I suggest, speaks to reliability in this inquiry is that *all the data underlined by the student-collaborators were accounted for and addressed in the chapters.* Triangulation was achieved at the expense of limiting the data to be interpreted, a practice that might be controvertial. But if the students thought it was important, I believe each datum has to be addressed. Picking and choosing from otherwise reduced data would compromise reliability and, perhaps, validity as well. The text would be less cooperatively evolved. Tyler (1986) is critical of some ethnographers who

> ...have tamed the savage, not with the pen but with the tape recorder, reducing him to a "straight man"...for even as they think to have returned to "oral performance" or "dialogue," in order that the native have a place in the text, they exercise control over her discourse and steal the only thing she has left—her voice. (p. 128)

To return to the question of reliability, however, would a different analyst make the same kind of interpretations of the data and arrive at the same conclusions? This is the question that has stirred up a great deal of controversy among anthropologists. Note the bitter reactions to Derek Freeman's (1983) criticism of Margaret Mead's work in Samoa (Howard, 1984). The question of reliability, I suppose, cannot be fully answered without a replication of the study. Until that happens, ethnographic inquiries might be evaluated by other means. In 1931, Alfred Kroeber, one of America's greatest anthropologists, wrote a review of Margaret Mead's *Growing Up in New Guinea* (1930) without having been there himself. Clifford (1988) quotes the review as an example of Kroeber's approval of Mead's ability to create "a common meaningful world" (p. 36). Long before Tyler's call for "post-modern ethnography," Kroeber wrote of Mead's book:

> The result is a representation of quite extraordinary vividness and semblance to life. Obviously, a gift of intellectualized but strong sensationalism underlies this capacity; also, obviously, a high order of intuitiveness, in the sense of the ability to complete a convincing picture from clues, for clues is all that some of her data can be, with only six months to learn a language and enter the inwards of a whole culture, besides specializing in child behavior. (p. 248)

Coming from Kroeber, a man who was fluent in many Native American languages, this was high praise, indeed, and it recognizes that the "convincing" picture presented by the text often outweighs the nagging questions. Mead's text took on a life of its own. The fragments of discourse that form the basic data for our study can only give clues. Young people from the subject population decided what the important clues were. The writing fills in the spaces between the fragments in an attempt to complete a cohesive picture. The reader has access to all the underlined data and can decide if the picture completed from those clues is convincing.

Recalling the Literature

In the course of writing, I attempted to bring in other theorists, researchers, and educators whose writings elucidate, expand, explain, or support the findings. The connections came out of my memory, jogged by the dialogue. The book, of course, does not begin with a review of literature which is then referred to in the course of the narrative. If we attempt to have the theory come out of the data, we must start with the data rather than the literature. In a traditional hypothesis study, the hypothesis supposedly comes out of the prior literature so a review of previous research is appropriate. Freud (1927) did a marvelous review of literature in *The Interpretation of Dreams* but did not refer back to it very often in the course of his narrative.

Except for Berger and Luckmann, Bowers, Bruner, Erickson, Erikson, Everhart, Fine, Gergen, Glaser and Strauss, Illich and Sanders, Lather, Oakley, Patai, Sullivan, and Tyler, none of the numerous other authors I have cited were used to directly frame or to introduce the book. All of the other researchers or commentators arose because of the relationship of their work to the data of the study, *after the fact and because I made the connection.* The process of the writing of the final text as well as the text itself takes on a life of its own. But even though I am that writer, the text is driven by data; no data, no book.

The book, then, is a type of ethnographic inquiry, even if it does not meet everyone's definition of ethnography. It creates a picture of a "possible" world and, hopefully, will inform education and will increase practitioners', researchers', and policymakers' understanding of the symbolic universes of inner-city students. The methodology is very appropriate, I suggest, for some inquiries but less so for others. I believe education can profit from it. But according to Ricouer, of course, this text, upon completion, will be detached from me and develop consequences of its own. I cannot predict what those consequences will be.

References

Assembly of God Churches. (1934). *Tenets of Faith of the Assembly of God Churches*. Springfield, Mo.: Author.

Baldwin, J. M. (1897). *Social and Ethical Implications of Mental Development*. New York: Macmillan.

Baumrind, D. (1973). "The Development of Instrumental Competence through Socialization." In A. D. Dick (ed.), *Minnesota Symposium on Child Psychology* (vol. 7). Minneapolis: University of Minnesota Press.

Beck, R., and Wood, D. (1993). "The Dialogic Socialization of Aggression in a Family's Court of Reason and Inquiry." *Discourse Processes* 16; 271–93.

Beit-Hallahimi, B. (1973). Editor's introduction. In B. Beit Hallahimi (ed.), *Research in Religious Behavior: Selected Readings*. Monterey, Calif.: Wadsworth.

Berger, P., and Luckmann, T. (1967). *The Social Construction of Reality: A Treatise in the Sociology of Knowledge*. New York: Doubleday.

Bernstein, B. (1970). "A Sociolinguistic Approach to Socialization, with Some Reference to Educability." In F. Williams (ed.), *Language and Poverty: Perspectives on a Theme*. Chicago: Markham.

Beteille, A. (1967). "The Future of the Backward Classes: The Competing Demands of Status and Power." In P. Mason (ed.), *India and Ceylon: Unity and Diversity* (pp. 83–120). New York: Oxford.

Blase, J. J. (1986). "Socialization as Humanization: One Side of Being a Teacher." *Sociology of Education*, 59: 100–113.

Book, C., and Freeman, D. (1986). "Differences in Early Characteristics of Elementary and Secondary Teacher Candidates." *Journal of Teacher Education*, 37(2): 47–51.

Bourdieu, P. (1986). "The Production of Belief: Contribution to an Economy of Symbolic Goods." *Media, Culture, and Society* 2: 261–93.

Bowers, C. A. (1984). *The Promise of Theory: Education and the Politics of Social Change*. New York: Longman.

Bowker, G. (1968). *The Education of Coloured Immigrants*. New York: Humanities Press.

Braithwaite, E. R. (1968). "The 'colored immigrant' in Britain." In J. H. Franklin (ed.), *Color and Race* (pp. 218–83). Boston: Houghton-Mifflin.

Bruner, J. (1986). *Actual Minds, Possible Worlds*. Cambridge: Harvard.

Bruner, J. (1987). "Prologue to the English Edition." In R. W. Reiber and A. S. Carton (eds.), *The Collected Works of L. S. Vygotsky*, Vol. 1, *Problems of General Psychology*; (pp. 1–16). New York: Plenum.

Bruner, J. (1990). *Acts of Meaning*. Cambridge: Harvard.

Carew, J. V., and Lightfoot, S. L. (1979). *Beyond Bias: Perspectives on Classrooms*. Cambridge: Harvard.

Central Park East Secondary School. (1991). *Senior Institute Handbook*. New York City Board of Education: Author.

Children's Defense Fund. (1988). *A Children's Reform Budget: FY 1988*. Washington, D.C.: Author.

Clark, K. B. (1963). *Prejudice and Your Child*. Boston: Beacon Press.

Clifford, J. (1988). *The Predicament of Culture: Twentieth-Century Ethnography, Literature, and Art*. Cambridge: Harvard.

Dewey, J. (1897). "My Pedagogic Creed." *The School Journal* 54, 3: 77–80.

Dewey, J. (1963). *Experience and Education*. New York: Collier (original work published 1938).

Eckert, P. (1989). *Jocks and Burnouts: Social Categories and Identity in the High School*. New York: Teachers College Press.

El-Amin, Y. B. (1992). "Autobiography." Unpublished paper. The City College, City University of New York.

Erickson, F. (1986). "Qualitative Methods in Research on Teaching." In M. Whitrock (ed.), *Handbook in Research in Teaching* (3d ed., pp. 119–61). New York: Macmillan.

Erikson, E. H. (1963). *Childhood and Society*. New York: Norton.

Erikson, E. H. (1968). *Identity: Youth and Crisis*. New York: Norton.

Everhart, R. (1977). "Between Stranger and Friend: Some Consequences of 'long term' Fieldwork in Schools." *American Educational Research Journal* 25: 1–15.

Farrell, E. (1986). "Initiation into the Tabernacle: Enculturation in a Pentecostal Church." Paper presented at the Sixth Annual Ethnography in Education Research Forum, University of Pennsylvania.

Farrell, E. (1990). *Hanging in and Dropping out: Voices of At-Risk High School Students*. New York: Teachers College Press.

Farrell, E.; Peguero, G.; Lindsey, R.; and White, R. (1988). "Giving Voice to High School Students: Pressure and Boredom, Ya Know What I'm Sayin'?" *American Educational Research Journal* 25: 489–502.

Fauconnier, G. (1985). *Mental Spaces: Aspects of Meaning Construction in Natural Language*. Cambridge: MIT Press.

Fine, M. (1985). "Dropping out of High School: An Inside Look." *Social Policy* 16 (2): 43–50.

Fine, M. (1986). "Why Urban Adolescents Drop out of Public High School." *Teachers College Record* 87: 393–409.

Fine, M. (1987). "Silencing in Public Schools." *Language Arts* 64: 157–74.

Fine, M. (1991). *Framing Dropouts: Notes on the Politics of an Urban Public High School*. Albany, NY: State University of New York Press.

Fine, M., and Rosenberg, P. (1983). "Dropping out of High School: The Ideology of School and Work." *Journal of Education* 165: 257–72.

Foley, D. E. (1991). *Learning Capitalist Culture: Deep in the Heart of Tejas*. Philadelphia: University of Pennsylvania Press.

Freeman, D. (1983). *Margaret Mead and Samoa: The Making and Unmaking of an Anthropological Myth*. Cambridge: Harvard.

Freud, S. (1927). *The interpretation of dreams*. Translated by A. A. Powell. London: George Allen and Unwin (original work published in 1900).

Gardner, H. (1983). *Frames of Mind: The Theory of Multiple Intelligences*. New York: Basic Books.

Gergen, K. J. (1967). *To Be or Not to Be a Single Self: Existential Perspectives on the Self*. Gainesville: University of Florida Press.

Gergen, K. J. (1972). "Multiple Identity: The Healthy Happy Human Being Wears Many Masks." *Psychology Today* 5: 31–35, 64–66.

Getzels, J. W., and Jackson, P. W. (1963). "The Teacher's Personality and Characteristics." In N. L. Gage (ed.), *Handbook of Research on Teaching* (pp. 506–58). Chicago: Rand-McNally Co.

Gibson, M. A. (1988). *Accommodation without assimilation: Punjabi Sikh Immigrants in an American High School and Community*. Ithaca: Cornell University Press.

Gilligan, C. (1977). "In a Different Voice: Women's Conceptions of Self and Morality. *Harvard Educational Review* 47: 481–517.

Gilligan, C. (1982). *In a Different Voice: Psychological Theory and Women's Development*. Cambridge: Harvard University Press.

Glaser, B., and Strauss, A. (1967). *The Discovery of Grounded Theory: Strategies for Qualitative Research*. Chicago: Aldine.

Goleman, D. (1992, April 21). "Black Scientists Study the 'pose' of the Inner City." *The New York Times*, C1.

Goodenow, C. (1992). "Strengthening the Links between Educational Psychology and the Study of Social Contexts." *Educational Psychologist* 27: 177–96.

Goodman, P. (1968, May 18). "Freedom and Learning: The Need for Choice." *Saturday Review* 73.

Gould, S. J. (1981). *The Mismeasure of Man*. New York: Norton.

Hine, V. (1969). "Pentecostal Glossalia—Toward a Fuctional Interpretation." *Journal for the Scientific Study of Religion* 8: 211–26.

Howard, J. (1984). *Margaret Mead: A Life*. New York: Fawcett.

Illich, I., and Sanders, B. (1988). *A B C: The Alphabetation of the Popular Mind*. New York: Vintage.

Indire, F. F. (1969, September). "Motives Inspiring Secondary School Teachers." *Teachers College News* (Nairobi, Kenya).

Inhelder, B., and Piaget, J. (1958). *The Growth of Logical Thinking from Childhood to Adolescence*. New York: Basic Books.

Jackson, P. W. (1968). *Life in Classrooms*. New York: Holt, Rinehart, and Winston.

James, W. (1902). *The Varieties of Religious Experience*. London: Longmans.

Kagan, J. (1984). *The Nature of the Child*. New York: Basic Books.

Kohlberg, L. (1981). *The Philosophy of Moral Development*. Vol.1, *Moral Stages and the Idea of Justice*. New York: Harper and Row.

Kozol, J. (1991). *Savage Inequalities: Children in America's Schools*. New York: Crown.

Kroeber, A. (1931). "Review of *Growing up in New Guinea*, by Margaret Mead." *American Anthropologist* 36: 248.

Kunjufu, J. (1985). *Countering the Conspiracy to Destroy Black Boys*. Chicago: African-American Publishing Company.

Lakoff, G. (1985). In G. Fauconnier, *Mental Spaces: Aspects of Meaning Construction in Natural Language*. Cambridge: MIT Press.

Lather, P. (1991). *Geting Smart: Feminist Research and Pedagogy with/in the Postmodern*. New York: Routledge.

Lee, F. R. (1990, February 12). "Trying Times for Guidance Counselors." *The New York Times*, B1,4.

Lee, V., and Eckstrom, R. (1987). "Student Access to Guidance Couseling in High School." *American Educational Research Journal* 24: 287-310.

LeVine, R. A. (1967). *Dreams and Needs: Achievement Motivation in Nigeria*. Chicago: University of Chicago Press.

Lightfoot, S. L. (1983). *The Good School*. New York: Basic Books.

Lortie, D. C. (1975). *Schoolteachers: A sociological study*. Chicago: University of Chicago Press.

Luria, A. R. (1987). "Afterward." In R. W. Reiber and A. S. Carton (eds.), *The Collected Works of L. S. Vygotsky*. Vol. 1, *Problems of General Psychology* (pp. 359-73). New York: Plenum.

Markus, H., and Nurius, P. (1986). "Possible Selves." *American Psychologist* 41: 954-69.

Masling, J., and Stern, G. (1966). *The Pedagogical Significance of Unconscious Factors in Career Motivation for Teachers*. (Project No. 512). Washington, D.C.: U.S. Office of Education (Dept. of H.E.W. Research Project No. SAE 8175).

Mead, G. H. (1922). "A Behavioristic Account of the Significant Symbol." *The Journal of Philosophy* 29: 157-68.

Mead, G. H. (1934). *Mind, Self, and Society: From the Standpoint of a Social Behaviorist*. Chicago: University of Chicago Press.

Mead, M. (1930). *Growing up in New Guinea: A Comparative Study of Primitive Education*. New York: Blue Ribbon Books.

Meier, D. (1992). "Reinventing Teaching." *Teachers College Record* 93: 594-609.

National Center for Education Statistics. (1990). *Digest of Educational Statistics*. Washington, D.C.: Government Printing Office.

Neill, A. S. (1960). *Summerhill: A Radical Approach to Childrearing*. New York: Hart.

Oakley, A. (1981). "Interviewing Women: A Contradiction in Terms." In H. Roberts (ed.), *Doing Feminist Research* (pp. 30–61). Boston: Routledge and Kegan Paul.

Ogbu, J. U. (1978). *Minority Education and Caste: The American System in a Cross-Cultural Perspective*. Orlando, Fla.: Academic Press.

Ogbu, J. U. (1989). "Cultural Models and Educational Strategies of Non-Dominant Peoples." *The 1989 Catherine Molony Memorial Lecture*. New York: The City College Workshop Center.

O'Hare, W. P.; Pollard, K. M.; Mann, T. L.; and Kent, M. M. (1991). "African Americans in the 1990's." *Population Bulletin* 46: 1. Washington, D.C.: Population Reference Bureau, Inc. (July).

Opie, I., and Opie, P. (1959). *The Lore and Language of Schoolchildren*. London: Oxford University Press.

Parsons, T. (1955). "Family Structure and the Socialization of the Child." In T. Parsons and R. F. Bales (eds.), *Family, Socialization, and Interaction Process*. New York: Free Press.

Patai, D. (1988). "Constructing a Self: A Brazilian Life Story." *Feminist Studies* 14: 143–66.

Piaget, J. (1950). *The Psychology of Intelligence*. Translated by M. Piercy and D. E. Berlyne. London: Routledge and Kegan Paul.

Piaget, J. (1965). *The Moral Judgment of the Child*. New York: Basic Books (original published in 1932).

Pittman, K. (1988). In T. Lewin (March 20). "Fewer Teen Mothers, but More are Unmarried." *New York Times*, 6.

Pollak, S., and Gilligan, C. (1982). "Images of Violence in Thematic Apperception Test Stories." *Journal of Personality and Social Psychology* 42: 159–67.

Powell, A.; Farrar, E.; and Cohen, D. (1985). *The Shopping Mall High School: Winners and Losers in the Educational Marketplace*. Boston: Houghton Mifflin.

Ricouer, P. (1981). *Hermeneutics and the Human Sciences*. Edited and translated by J. B. Thompson. New York: Cambridge.

Rose, E. J. (1969). *Colour and Citizenship: A Report on British Race Relations*. New York: Oxford.

Shibutani, T. (1961). *Society and Personality: An Interactionist Approach to Social Psychology*. Englewood Cliffs, N.J.: Prentice Hall.

Sullivan, H. S. (1953). *The Interpersonal Theory of Psychiatry*. New York: Norton.

Toulmin, S. E. (1963). *The Uses of Argument*. Cambridge: Cambridge University Press.

Tyler, S. (1986). "Post-Modern Ethnography: From Document of the Occult to Occult Document." In J. Clifford and G. Marcus (eds.), *Writing Culture: The Poetics and Politics of Ethnography* (pp. 122–64). Berkeley: University of California Press.

Vygotsky, L. S. (1987). "The Problem of Will and Its Development in Childhood." In R. W. Rieber and A. S. Carton (eds.), *The Collected Works of L. S. Vygotsky.* Vol. 1, *Problems in General Psychology* (pp. 351–58). New York: Plenum.

Wilson, W. J. (1987). *The Truly Disadvantaged: The Inner City, the Underclass, and Public Policy.* Chicago: University of Chicago Press.

Wood, D., and Beck, R. (1993). *Home Rule: Culture, Environment and the American Family.* Baltimore: Johns Hopkins University Press.

Index